The Single Parent's Guide
to Raising Godly Children

BOOKS BY SHAE COOKE

Reflections on The Shack

Reflections on 90 Minutes in Heaven

Reflections From the Powder Room on The Love Dare

Pina Coladas and the Pearly Gates

Will My Pet Go to Heaven?

Beautiful One

AVAILABLE FROM DESTINY IMAGE PUBLISHERS

The Single Parent's Guide to Raising Godly Children

The Single Parent's Guide Series

SHAE COOKE

DESTINY IMAGE® PUBLISHERS, INC.
P.O. Box 310, Shippensburg, PA 17257-0310

"Speaking to the Purposes of God for This Generation and for the Generations to Come."

This book and all other Destiny Image, Revival Press, MercyPlace, Fresh Bread, Destiny Image Fiction, and Treasure House books are available at Christian bookstores and distributors worldwide.

For a U.S. bookstore nearest you, call 1-800-722-6774.
For more information on foreign distributors, call 717-532-3040.
Or reach us on the Internet: www.destinyimage.com.

Trade Paper ISBN 13: 978-0-7684-3198-8
Hardcover ISBN 13: 978-0-7684-3458-3
Large Print ISBN 13: 978-0-7684-3459-0
Ebook ISBN 13: 978-0-7684-9110-4

For Worldwide Distribution, Printed in the U.S.A.
1 2 3 4 5 6 7 8 / 14 13 12 11 10

God never promised us an easy life...only that it would be outstandingly worth it!

Contents

Foreword

There is very little in today's world that is more difficult than raising children in a single-parent home. Yet surprisingly, there are few resources for single parents.

It has always been the mission of Destiny Image to speak to the Church about what is on God's heart. Over the years this mission has taken on many shapes, often by publishing authors that most—if not all—other Christian publishers would never touch. Women, African Americans, preachers from third world countries, small town pastors, and many others who simply heard a word from the Lord. God is no respecter of persons, and He can speak through anyone, as long as we are willing to hear.

This book had its birth on an ordinary Tuesday afternoon. A random newsletter popped up in my email, and just as I was about to hit "delete," a phrase in the headline caught my eye: "Single Parent's Conference." Now, I am not a single parent, but I was intrigued. I had felt for many months that God was trying to speak a new direction to me, and that I was simply missing what it was supposed to be. This phrase sparked something in my spirit, and I opened the email.

At first glance, the idea of a conference for single parents was exciting to me. *Finally,* I thought, *the church is catching up to the times and not treating single parents like pariahs.* But then I read a little further: This was a 3-day conference. Three days seemed a bit much to me, but I kept reading: Registration was $400. Again, a bit of a commitment for a single parent. And then the kicker: *No child care provided.*

So here was a conference intended to help single parents, yet it contained three major barriers to single parents actually being able to attend! What single parent can afford to take three days off work, pay $400, and *still* have to find a babysitter for the duration of the conference? None that I know.

I knew there had to be a better way to help single parents. After all, they have one of the hardest jobs in the world today, and some of the weakest support structures. Most churches still try to pretend that every family is like the Cleavers. Single mothers especially have a hard time finding acceptance, and their children are treated like they have some kind of disease.

And so this book—and an entire series of books like this one—began to take shape. Never having been a single parent, I was not about to consider myself qualified to write a book on the subject. But being in the publishing industry gave me a great head start—I just happened to have an entire list of writers on my desk.

Armed with an outline, a book proposal, and comments from many single parents that help make the mission of Destiny Image a reality, I sent an email to Shae Cooke.

And now you hold *The Single Parent's Guide to Raising Godly Children* in your hands.

Jonathan Nori, Vice President
Destiny Image, Inc.

INTRODUCTION

Ice Is Hard to Fry—
Single Parenting Isn't Easy

I daresay that no crooked table legs or ill-fitted drawers ever came out of the carpenter's shop in Nazareth
—Dorothy Leigh Sayers[1]

Before I joined The Hood, I was a perfect parent in spirit—boy, patient as a turtle and as stress free as a butterflied shrimp on ice. I had all the formulas, secrets, straightforward plans, and opinions for success in raising happy, healthy, respectful, godly, obedient, and politely mannered children who would always behave in restaurants and supermarkets, always be mindful of their p's and q's, and consistently be asking, "What would Jesus do" when they had the urge to smear regurgitated squash on the walls. No child of mine would ever tantrum at the checkout because he wanted a chocolate bar, or eat a junk dog for lunch, play Xbox twelve hours straight, or go three days without brushing his teeth. Nor would I ever wear sweatpants, pull my hair through a scrunchie, or go anywhere with a five-month old manicure.

Nor would I ever be going it…alone.

Can we talk about the best laid plans of God? Our Parent-in-Chief's plan is to prosper us, not to harm us, and to give us a hope and a future.[2] Thankfully, God the Father does not look for reasons to punish His people for being imperfect, nor does He banish us. God knows especially how complicated our lives are. It is good to know that He knows and keeps up on current events.

Out of *Zoom*

I almost think that having it all together is a waste of God's grace. The fact is, many of us strive toward perfection, try to go from zero to 60, and feel frustrated when we lose the *zoom* or wonder why we make mistakes. I have decided that I simply cannot be amazing at everything or be everything to everyone, including my son.

Our home has its share of fussing, complaining, mumbling, grumbling, whining, slammed doors, arguments, tears, and meltdowns—and much dust, dog hair, and fossilized snot. Hey, I blow my witness (and credibility) daily. And hey again—sometimes DS (Dear Son) looks like an extra on "Oliver Twist." But I've learned that I have to let go of some things to focus on what is important, like spending time with DS who is growing up so quickly and needs me. He has been through *so* much through *no fault of his own*. Vulnerable, the world wants him, and it's got him to a degree. Something has to give, and I prefer to slack on the things that really do not matter rather than take time away from him. Why? Because he needs love and time, and he equates time as love and acceptance. Better he finds love and acceptance from me or his father.

Pencil in Some Free Time

_____

_____

_____

_____

_____

Ha, ha, ha.

My, How Time Flies

Relationally, DS, now 13 (he was 8 when his dad and I split up) and I have an unbreakable bond, and while in each milestone of his life I have seen gain, I have also perceived a little loss, in the sense of "You're not cool Mom," and "Puh. What E-VER!"

Now that he is not a "kid" anymore, sometimes I think I just don't know DS as well as I once did, often asking myself, _who is he?_ Yesterday he was 4'3"—today he is 5'11". Suddenly I am living with a child giant who can physically take me out with a flick of his pinky if his foot odor doesn't face-plant me first. Crackly voice, fuzzy mustache, quirky language—who knew these pubescent years could be so interestingly different and yet strangely the same. Out of the sandbox and into Xbox. And still into the single syllables: "Uh-uh. Yup. Not." I'm comfortable with it.

Not, never.

Oh I yearn to explain to DS all the complexities of trying to be a good parent, never mind a single one, so that perhaps he can better understand my motivations. Today, he tunes out every one of my "If I told you once, I've told you a thousand times..." And to his credit...good on him! That would be called "nagging," and nagging is not good. Obviously I have some 'splaining to do.

While I *have* built a biblical foundation to the best of my ability, he does stray from it, particularly when at school or at his father's house. I worry that perhaps I didn't build it strong enough, wide enough, or long enough. *"Train [a] a child in the way he should go, and when he is old he will not turn from it"*[3] scares me silly sometimes. What if I don't do it all or right? What if I fail?

DS knows I am not perfect, and reminds me daily! The fact that I am *not* God is to his benefit. It gives him permission to be imperfect too. He delights in my imperfections...in the same way that my Jack Russell Terrier, Grace, romps in bear poop. My blemishes give DS the dreaded "edge." You know, bargaining power. Laud it over me power. "Mom, like you are so *totally* a liar!"

When Being the Star of the Show Is *Not* So Good

The greatest actors I know are single parents who daily put up brave, strong, fearless fronts. However, in truth and in secret before God, alone at night with thoughts, incognito in parenting chat rooms, blogs and forums, in journals, or in the bathroom, most admit or lament at least occasional bouts of fear, anxiety, worry, guilt, hopelessness.

My pillow, if it could talk, would attest to the times I have buried my head in it and cried, "I CAN'T TAKE IT ANYMORE!" It would expose me as a sometimes weak, vulnerable, fearful, and worried parent. What do I worry about the most? My inability to erase the hurt in DS's precious, gorgeous eyes. My desperation to tell little white lies to stop his confused tears. My sympathy toward him that results in my excusing his disrespectful behavior because of what we, his parents, have put him through. My desire to never let him gain access to the world but—*sigh*—knowing that it is inevitable.

Some days I go full throttle, Mazda *zoom zoom* I can handle everything; but other days I'm a candidate for the Cash for Clunkers program: *S-c-r-e-e-c-h!* "You *still* want that Mohawk?" "How did that marble get up your nose?" "No your ear is not an extra pocket from God." "Does that wash off?" "What's my purse doing in the toilet?" "Did you tell your father what I did?" "Rent is going up, how much?" "Can you pass me that flashlight, I'm sure I paid that bill." "She's *how* old?"

I am who I am, an imperfect God-passionate at times lonely and often materially, physically, and spiritually spent parent in the throes of trying to raise a God-passionate, firmly anchored, well-adjusted, obedient child in the bewildering confusion of our time.

Some people call me brave, but I presume that is a code word for "Thank goodness I'm not wearing your imitation Pradas." I also suspect I'm used as a red flag by bony-fingered finger-pointing folk—"See what happens when you make wrong choices?" Sure I long for the day when the Extreme Makeover Home Edition crew pulls up to our door, and for that cutie television show host Ty to shriek through his megaphone: "Good morning Cooke family!" Then he and his workers will build us a dream house, "just because!" But I place greater faith in God, who is much more reliable as the Fulfiller of Dreams beyond my craziest hopes. If I believe what Jesus taught, I know that the answers to my practical questions about finances, child rearing, and all the obligations I have, begin and end with my Source for Truth, found in and for me.

The intangibles are much more important than the tangibles. You can't put a price on a miracle of God. I have since learned to put everything in God's basket-like hands, to be satisfied with what I have, and to stay away from pyramid parties, Nigerian email offers, and, in short, from trying to create my own miracles. But I have to say, Craigslist and eBay are amazing resources for the financially-strapped parent!

Disheartening Stats as Opportunity

Almost every researched work I see blames the single parent situation for the uptrend in children-gone-bad stats and other social problems. That is depressing, especially since I know many single parents—the "oops I blew its," widowed, divorced, spiritually separated, and separated by distance—raising amazing and godly children on their own. And I mean "on their own," save for God in their midst, and doing it brilliantly in partnership with Him—better than most non-believing dual parent families.

In my opinion, statistics citing single parents and their offspring are much too unfair and imbalanced. Perhaps such numbers reflect unbelieving families who have no hope in transformation and the day-to-day presence, guidance, and intervention of God in their lives. (Do not abandon such research though—discern and use findings for the good to help you identify vulnerabilities, assess the true risks and opportunities, and take appropriate action.)

We need to see more studies of single families and their offspring doing things right! How about headlines that one day read:

Widower Mom of Five Adopting Two Haitian Orphans in Aftermath of Devastating Quake

Seven-year-old Son of Single Mother Starts Anti-Bullying Campaign at School

Single Parent-Led Families Descend on Washington to Fight for Media Reform

Solo Dad of Three Works Two Jobs, Raises $1 Million for New Senior Home

Seventeen-year-old Teen Returns Found Wallet Containing $1,000, on Advice of His Single Dad

Girl, 14, Daughter of a Single Mother, Inspires Classmates to "Wait"

Who says only dual-parent families can forge important trails? Who says my child cannot become a history maker? Who says we cannot be cohesive, deeply rooted, and grounded families with much to contribute to church, society, and the Kingdom of God?

I refuse the negative status quo and rebuke it—I do not give it a place in our home. My child will not be a sociopath or a misfit; he will not be misguided, abandoned, or abused.

Singleness Reality

Being a single parent is not cause for shame, does not mean I have deserted my post, or that I am unfaithful to my parental responsibilities. I did not choose singleness, and most of us do not—we embrace the sanctity of family as God intended it to be. My goodness, I grew up in an era of Dick and Jane ideals—the Mommy loves Daddy, buttercups in jars on the windowsill, tuck the kids in, say their prayers—whole and wholesome have-your-cake-and-apple-pie-family dream! I didn't have it as a child, mind you, but this is what I dreamed for my family, and for the one I might have.

What a shocker it was the day my son and I ran down the street to the neighbor's house with little else than my purse, my Bible (my son's idea), and Mr. Bear (my idea) in tow. Our lives fell apart—but I did not quit loving, mothering, or caring for him. I did not give up my calling to raise DS in the way that he should go, and God did not desert me in that effort. Our blessings have been enormous in the face of crisis. I attribute that to the coming to the end of myself and the striving to control the events in my life so I could finally arrive at the place where I could say, "Lord, I surrender. Please take full control of my life."

Good Fear?

The entrance to DS's heart is more complex than the answer to "Why is there an expiration date on sour cream?" Unconditional love is the key that has helped me access that place for God's transforming and permeating power. DS's life does not depend on my receiving the answer to "why," but to receiving God's life-changing love power and choosing to trust that God is good, all the time. God restores, He brings healing and inner peace, He can help us learn and grow in the midst of the hottest fires of loss, and most of all, He is the answer to all that I seek.

God did not cause our situation. He doesn't break up homes. God makes all things work together for good, with good plans, not evil plans, for those who believe in Him and who are called according to His purposes. (See Romans 8:28.) He wants to give us a victorious future and hope for each day. This I know, because I have experienced the good and I have much hope!

Bad circumstances, disappointments, and even my fears exposed my lack of leaning on and trusting in God and in Him alone to transform things. As a result, I determined to reestablish and re-ground myself in His love, and when I did, it wasn't about what *I could not* do but about what *God could* do. Effective parenting is not so much about performance as it is about establishing and grounding ourselves in Christ! The greatest encouragement I can give is to keep Christ and His teachings as the absolute authority in your home, because He can overcome every obstacle that single parent's face.

Today I do regular foundation checks in my life to see where I really put my trust—upon whom I really lean, upon whose ability I truly rely as I seek to build upon the foundation I have laid for DS.

A Valuable Reality

Will grace cover omissions? Feelings of condemnation and inadequacy and fear of failure assailed me, especially in the evenings as I lay awake surveying the day. How I craved to be able to say, "It is finished," and mean it. To have the sense of accomplishment, of finishing well and successfully, with surety in my spirit that I had made a positive difference in DS's life, in his growth and in his training. That I'd done enough, said enough, listened enough, prayed enough, given enough, parented enough, and modeled enough. There were many l-o-n-g and painful nights of feeling as if I had failed in every vital department, and I half expected God to revoke my parenting privilege! "That's it, you're fired, Shae!"

The Lord showed me that the question is not about having a perfect family, for there is no such thing, nor is there a perfect or succinct parenting method that fits all families or each individual child equally. It is not about doing it all, being everything, shaping perfect children, crossing all the t's, dotting all the i's, but about embracing and treasuring the perfect love of God in our lives[4] and parenting from that most valuable reality.

Our parenting should mirror the profound relationship we have with God. As our children find their way toward their own faith, we move slowly and steadily toward greater knowledge of them, growing in wisdom and empathy while they grow into their own faith in size, strength of character, and perfect fearless love.

While the enemy hurls his potshots at my imperfections and causes me to obsess about whether I am doing or accomplishing, God simply asks, "Did you parent today in love?" If the perfect love of God through Christ who dwells in my heart by faith grounds me, the spotlight question is, "Did I do the loving things?"

I Have More Than Enough

No matter what we've lost or stand to lose, no matter what we have suffered or what we will suffer, no matter how bad our present circumstances or how bleak the outlook, if DS and I still have Jesus and nothing else but Jesus, that is more than enough. That's tougher said than done when our physical needs are so plentiful, when I have to put food on the table, when we even depend on community to assist us.

But Jesus is to be so precious to us that even if we lost everything—family, friends, community help—yet had our Jesus, we should still be able to truly and honestly say, "I can hardly believe how blessed we are!" This is how wonderful Jesus Christ should be to each of us, "*What is more, I consider everything a loss compared to the surpassing greatness of knowing Christ Jesus my Lord, for whose sake I have lost all things. I consider them rubbish, that I may gain Christ*" (Phil. 3:8).

God's Word got me through the rough beginnings and continues to see me through each day. Especially the Psalms, as I relate to David's heart and God's plan for his life.

I never stop believing that He has a plan for me, for DS, even for his father, because God is so much bigger than our circumstances. I knew one day that God could restore all that was lost to us, and eventually use us, as imperfect as we are, to become all that He intends.

We are not just surviving, but actually thriving in His grace and mercy. What the world calls luck, I call blessings from God. In our home there is no such thing as coincidence, but God-incidents.

I still fear. It rises occasionally…okay, like every day a second here or a moment there, but how I deal with it is different. I don't let it grab me by the tail and swing me around or claw at our family destiny. My lungs don't heave and my knees don't buckle nearly as much as they did when I first entered the territory of Splitzville. Now I can walk toward what frightens me most—being unable to care for DS, being unloved, and being alone; and, once the fur settles, I can see an amazing future awaiting us. Meow. I'm content. It's all God's doing. And I'm about to share how God will help your family thrive, too.

PART I

Moving Out of Dysfunction Junction—*Getting Yourself Together*

CHAPTER 1

Broken Home? Them's Fightin' Words!—*Think Victory, Not Oy!*

The happiest moments of my life have been the few which I have passed at home in the bosom of my family. —Thomas Jefferson

Think victory, not vanquished. People may say that the single parent family spells d-y-s-f-u-n-c-t-i-o-n, but don't believe it or settle for that diagnosis or prognosis. There will be problems, to be sure. God did not promise that we would not have them. He *has* promised, however, that He is in the midst of them, and all things will work together for the good, if we love Him enough to entrust our family's care to Him.

God has called us to be a holy people even out of the burdens and wounds of our heart. He is a loving God who loves us despite our shortcomings, and He can create in our life a new and whole functional family through the power of the death and resurrection of His own Son.

27

Getting Out of the Victim Swamp

At the beginning of my single-parenting adventure, DS lived in a broken home with a broken parent—me. He didn't have a mother for the first two or so weeks—he had an overwrought, anxiety-filled, fearful adult living with him. Thankfully, God pulled me out of the victim swamp through the kindness and love of family and friends soon enough to see what was happening, and I immediately took steps to re-create a sense of "family." This disruption for a time, fractured DS's sense of security, and, I'm convinced, delayed his healing. All he could see and feel was what I was seeing and feeling—brokenness in relationships and connectivity. He had no figuratively safe walls to speak of while we lived in Dysfunction Junction, much less real walls, until I emerged from the ashes, mustered new resolve, and found new "digs" hidden in Christ.

As heartbreaking as the circumstances may be—and my heart goes out to those who hurt like I did—we need to somehow get it together, and quickly. So many of us are still in captivity, in deep affliction, grieving, and groping our way through the rubble, which is not good for our children. They should not have to wait for us to sort out our own lives. Even one week… goodness, one day of parenting disruption can harm them.

> We must wake ourselves up! Or somebody else will take our place, and bear our cross, and thereby rob us of our crown.—William Booth, Founder, Salvation Army

William Booth knew what he was talking about, having served the homeless, vulnerable, and disadvantaged for decades.

We may not be within God's ideal design for family,[5] but we can *choose* to live within His ideals of wholeness and victorious living by trusting and allowing Him to reshape and recreate our broken little nations into ones that confound and influence the world and bring glory and honor to His name.[6]

What You Can Do Now: We owe it to our children to get the help we need to start living again. If you have been in a funk and are unable to manage or cope as you once did, or if you sense depression that you cannot navigate or control, please seek immediate spiritual and/or emotional counseling, and come up for air. There is a reason why the airlines ask parents to put on their own oxygen masks first!

Safeguard: Avoid catching the highly infectious victim mentality by talking to God right away and on-the-spot.

Don't Despise Small Beginnings

God's purpose is to restore what you have lost and to reconstruct what has been broken down. What looks like ruin will be restored, rebuilt, realigned, and readjusted to God's original intent for your family's life. God will heal every place you have been hurt. He will heal your mind, your doubt, your reasoning, and your imagination. He will heal your emotions, your anger, bitterness, resentment, jealousy, and fear. He will heal your will and the confidence that has been devastated and hindered by hopelessness. Everything that keeps you broken, He will heal.

I'll never forget that first awful evening on our own. DS was sick with the flu, and we slept on a mattress on the floor of a neighbor's family room. Neither of us could stop crying. As I surveyed what was left in our lives, I prayed, "We have so little, what good can possibly come from all of this?"

This is exactly where God needed me to be—inquiring of Him. My inquiry eventually led to knowing that everything would be all right, that I was accepted and loved, and to a realization of my purpose, which ultimately has led our family into wholeness.

God wants you to arise (come into your being) and build your family as a fragrant memorial to Him. He will strengthen your hands for this good and purposeful work.

Power Up: Effective parenting comes out of *who you are* more than *what you do.*

What You Can Do Now: It is good to question God—it leads to His purpose and His involvement.

Exiled, Not Defiled

We were in exile—with few possessions, no security, and little confidence. But the good news is, for God's people, restoration historically follows a period of exile.

Like clay in the hand of a potter, so we were in God's hand. Our single-family makeup was not His originally designed intent or ideal, nor mine, but in His hand, He created and formed us into another pot of His divine design, shaping it as seems best to Him.[7] The original pot may have been spoiled, but the Potter took that very same clay and recreated a newly functional, perfect pot from it! Same clay, same wheel, same Potter, *new* design.

Power Up: Never borrow from the future. If you worry about what may happen tomorrow and it does not happen, you have worried in vain. If it does happen, you will worry twice! Today's trouble is enough for today![8]

Appropriating Restoration

There is much talk out there about God using cracked pots—but I'm here to tell you, God's desire is not that you walk around beat up and cracked, but instead, every bit whole.[9] I sense that God is more of a Restorer than He is a repairer just plugging up holes.

The principle of restoration is throughout His Word, where He restores double, fourfold, and sevenfold, where He restores what is violently taken away, restoring land, families, and lives. He restored Joseph's life, Moses' life, and the lives of the Israelites who had been enslaved. Job received twice as much as he owned before. You may just end up with 14,000 sheep, 6,000 camels, 1,000 yoke of oxen, and a thousand she-asses (yikes) before all is said and done (truly, it's there, check out Job 42:10,12). We have His promise that He will restore the years that the locusts have eaten, restore health, restore our souls, that He will renew a right spirit within us and restore our joy.

Why would He just tighten a screw, fix a wobbly leg, or apply a little spit and polish to our lives when He could give us a brand-new life—a brand new family, a whole new way of thinking, acting, and being? Listen, even if it is His plan to bring your spouse back to you, He will still make it new! He will restore you both with new love, romance, commitment, a new way to connect, and new resolve. He is a Carpenter through and through in the "good as new" business! Will you do what it takes to appropriate this Gospel of renewal in your life, in your family?

Put Your Right and Left Foot In

Restoration has two important steps, repentance and forgiveness, whether it is between you and God or you and another.

My friend Peter (not his real name) received a telephone call informing him that his wife, the mother of his four children, still babies and toddlers, had been shot and killed by a crazed lone gunman in the Dallas, Texas, halfway-house in which she volunteered. Beside himself with grief, justifiable rage, and a growing lust for revenge, he turned to his pastor, who immediately advised Peter, for his own sake and the sake of his small children, that the first step would be to forgive his wife's killer. Thrust suddenly into widowhood and into the role of a single parent, Peter needed to immediately gain control of his life through the power of forgiveness.

This is an extreme case; however, forgiveness looks the same no matter the injustice or cruelty dealt us. It is the most significant factor in our spiritual, psychological, and emotional healing—the core dynamic of who we are and where our journey will take us.

Jesus the Healer offered His life for the forgiveness of those who have harmed us. He set the perfect example of forgiveness in His dying breath. Never once did He seek vengeance in word or deed,[10] but prayed regarding those who crucified Him, *"Father forgive them, for they do not know what they do."*[11] Christ understood the evil potential of the human heart yielding to hostile, vengeful emotions,[12] something that divorced or separated single parents are especially at risk to do.

Had Peter not forgiven his wife's murderer, the bitterness, hatred, desire for revenge, could have caused serious emotional and physiological problems that would compound over time and increase the suffering of his entire family. Holding onto vengeful anger is like taking poison and waiting for someone else to die.[13]

What You Can Do Now: Do you need to forgive someone who has hurt you? Forgiveness is our most effective tool and response to single parenting, for the root of forgiveness is perfect love.

Straight Talk: Here's the thing. You need to willingly allow God to recreate your family in an image of His unique design in order for maximum effectiveness to occur. Be open to His new design and to even greater reliance on Him to fill the void left by the other parent. Put to death the possibility of terrible outcomes. Clothe your family with a brand-new and constantly renewing nature by together learning all you can about Christ, about the nature of God the Father who has His design on you. It doesn't matter that you are not the traditional family, since Christ is all who matters. If you each believe in Him, He lives in all of you, and His peace will rule and reign in your hearts, transforming upset into order and giving new and significant meaning to the term "family."

Power Up: Be encouraged! God is your co-parent—you cannot get better help anywhere.

26 Ways to Transform Upset Into Order

1. Use the word *family* often around your children.

2. Inquire of God for your family.

3. Call on godly friends to pray healing over you.

4.   Change your negative outlook.

5.   Take off old negative practices.

6.   Rid yourself of anger and resentment against your former spouse.

7.   Open the door to healthy relationships.

8.   Relate to your ex-spouse with grace and maturity.

9.   See the possibilities of your new situation from God's view (His Word and prayer).

10. Strengthen yourself in Christ.

11. Repent for mistrusting Him, if necessary, and for misleading your children.

12. Seek His forgiveness. Then let go of the guilt.

13. Forgive others. Release them to God.

14. Give Him permission to rework the clay.

15. Draw from His power.

16. Rise, and be healed.

17. Say, "I can cope because I have hope!"

18. Communicate forgiveness and release to your child by your words and actions.

19. Respect her individual and unique gifts and personalities.

20. Be yourself. Everyone else is taken!

21. Be authentic and willing to admit a weakness or a mistake, and to seek forgiveness.

22. Become passionate about God—this is what your child wants and needs.

23. Evaluate godly advice said privately in love. Other people can see things that you cannot, and may have great insight into parenting. If it is for your benefit, it may be worth listening to—their advice could be God speaking to you.

24. Immediately and regularly meditate on God's Word. Pastor Rick Warren says, "If you know how to worry, you already know how to meditate."[14] You need to be traveling ahead on the journey and preparing for your children's journey.

25. Sing a song unto the Lord.

26. Pray daily, discussing things with Him and listening for His heartfelt answers.

What Family Means to God

Families are not biological accidents or mere social constructs that can be discarded as irrelevant. They are important to God's plan, and He loves them just as much regardless of the structure or the shortcoming of the parents. He does not want your family to suffer the consequences, effects, or after-effects of your marital breakdown, loss, or dysfunction. Nor does He desire to punish you or your children, to see you bound up and brokenhearted, unable to function, or drowning in disadvantage. God places as great an importance on families whether a child is raised by one parent or two, by an aunt or an uncle, a grandparent, an orphanage, or by a foster parent.

God's love endures all things and does not change even if situations change. He did not reject my family because we were not in the perfect-case scenario. In compassion, He reached out to restore us with all-consuming, passionate, holy, jealous, and gentle love, continually offering forgiveness, comfort, encouragement, peace, joy, and His amazing power so that we *could* be the family of His perfect design. The Bible describes the attributes of a divinely whole family. Find it in Colossians 3:1-25. You will be amazed!

CHAPTER 2

Trouble to Trouble or Glory to Glory?—*How to Be a Power Perfect Single Parent*

Life should not be one trouble following another. In fact, our lives should grow from glory to glory.—Don Nori Sr.[15]

Power—we need much of it as single parents, and our kids do too, as their emotional needs rise and our responsibilities multiply. If you think solo parenting is a challenge, try being a child or young person today. It's a task just to stay innocent!

Single, working dads have to take on the additional role of housekeeping and nurturing, and moms have to take on the additional role of home maintenance and discipline and provide sole financial support, usually outside the home. Tell me again, how do I fix that leaky faucet? What's a wrench?

Not to mention the emotional shock of shattered dreams, helping our children adjust to trauma and change, additional worry that the absence of a helpmate might affect our children's physical, emotional, and spiritual well-beings and development—it can all be so wearisome. We know in our hearts that a one-parent home is not God's original design. What if we miss something the other parent could have given, provided, or done; what if we cannot possibly get it all accomplished solo. Be honest. We know this takes power we may not have alone.

Our Highest Priority

However, we also have this promise: If we *"seek first His kingdom [God and His Kingship over you] and His righteousness... **all** of these things will be given to you as well,"*[16] you will accrue the very best for your kids.

Jesus clearly established this as the highest-priority goal for His disciples and it is our highest priority as parents. Why? Because He knows that the main goal, our highest priority, determines the preparations, efforts, and zeal for reaching it. He also knows we need hope for the best outcomes possible for our family. We must prioritize God's kingship over us in our lives especially now, and pursue it with determination and expectancy if we don't want our children to miss out. This is our Plan A. There is no Plan B!

Powerless? Hopeless? Think Again!

Emmanuel, God is with you! I know sometimes it is hard to believe; I had my time of it. But God promises He will never leave or forsake you. His power for your life comes in that very hope in Him. Power without hope is not the kind of power you or your son or daughter need. You need the kind of power that can help you "see" which decisions and actions carry the best weight, consequences, and results. You need the kind of reviving power that helps you actually enjoy your child as a divine blessing. How awesome! You need the power of *"Do not worry about tomorrow, for tomorrow will worry about itself"* (Matt. 6:34).

When Being in the Dark is Good

Darkness is not a sign that God is not with us, even though I thought this was the case when my marriage dissolved and my son and I were homeless. "Lord, if You had been here when we called…Where were You? In fact, hello, where *are* You?"

As David of the Bible discovered when hemmed in by the enemy, God had made our darkness our hiding place in Him; and, in the background, He worked to split wide the way where there seemed to exist no way during black, turbulent times. Our hope in Him actually "declares to the world that we belong to Someone who stabilizes us in the midst of turbulence!"[17]

It is this hope that declares to the world and to our children that yes, we belong to God, that He loves to mend broken people, and that He saves us not because of the righteous things we have done, but because of His mercy.[18]

Don't Settle for Your Reality

"I'm dying here!"

"It's just too much!"

"You have no idea!"

"How will we get through to next month?"

"My children are too needy…"

"I don't have enough time…"

"My ex is destroying the children."

"I'm afraid of being alone."

"Who will love me now?"

My marriage dissolved in 60 seconds, but its troubles brewed for years. As a result, part of my faith died. If you have a failed marriage or have experienced a death, you know this is true; these things can cause a true faith crisis. I, as Martha did when Lazarus died, questioned Jesus' timing. "Lord, if You had been here when I called…where were You?" How often we pray or at least wonder it (see John 11:21).

Have you ever felt like you have collided at the intersection of faith and reality? The things we expect and pray for sometimes just don't match up with our reality. Calamity hits. We give up on seeking biblical answers and God's power, and settle for unsatisfying worldview pat answers, remedies, and solutions. Inside, our self-talk goes like this: "I'm afraid to hope, I'm afraid to experience more disappointment. I feel vulnerable."

For a season, I too felt this way—I didn't dare hope. I was in self-defense mode with God and felt powerless. Oh man, I didn't like feeling emotionally dead. Do you know what Jesus told Martha? "Believe *in the* Resurrection standing before you! It's not just a future hope. You don't have to be dead to see My power now."[19]

Divorce, separation, alienation, and rejection are deaths of sorts, and we feel the loss in the same way that we would in the actual death of a loved one. Any time there is death, there is heartbreak, loneliness, sorrow, fear, and grief for everyone involved. We all die somewhat inside.

The same resurrection power that raised Jesus from the dead empowers me to rise above the cloud that still lingers sometimes. I'm awakened by Christ's loving ~~pinch~~ challenge: "Calamity Jane, believe in Me. Don't wait for Me to work and resurrect you when you are dead and buried, ask Me for resurrection power, now!"

Ooh-la-la and la! Believe me, I asked Him all right! I needed that kind of hope-power in my role as a single mom—hurting, without a job, zip for savings, and *sans* the physical and emotional support of a husband. My son would need that hope, too, as he spun out of control, heartbroken, dejected, with a heart yearning for the warm fuzzies of a stable family life. You and your child need that hope, too.

Think Eternal **When...**

- *Think eternal when you discover that fossilized snot does not come off the walls without peeling off the paint.*

- *Think eternal when your latchkey kids experiment with eggs, marshmallows, and potatoes in the microwave!*

- *Think eternal when the principal calls to tell you that she caught your perfect baby bullying the new kid in class.*

- *Think eternal when you think you are at the end of your parenting rope, and oops, there it is!*

- *Think eternal when your child tells you she hates you for the third time in one day.*

Straight Talk: You do not have to endure the emotional toll of wrestling with thoughts of never feeling whole and of being alone, or the worry of getting from today's circumstances to better tomorrows. With Him, it is all possible.

Rise! Until we recognize who we already are in Christ, until we realize our place in the heavenly realm, until we can glimpse the finished work of the Cross manifested within us, we will fear frayed ropes, cliff edges, and the dreaded, children-alone-with-the-microwave scenario!

Yours is not an impossible task. You and your children were created to rise from the dead and blaze with glory at the end of time! Your family can draw from His resurrection power and blaze with glory *now*.

Your home *can* be a power house of the Lord, growing from glory to glory. You can forge amazing trails as a single parent, and your children can become megawatt Rat Zappers, Gospel Rappers, and Brilliant Beacons, not to mention microwave geniuses. It's good if you can believe it. This sounds supernatural, doesn't it? I have news for you. It is.

The "B" Word

Believing is key to victorious single parenting: *Believe* that the Lord Jesus Christ of Nazareth burst out of the tomb, that death could not contain Him, and that it cannot contain you or your children! *Believe* in the resurrection standing before you. *Believe* that you can do all things through Christ who strengthens you.

I could finish the book right here. Save the trees and all that. If you take anything away, take this truth (even though it sounds trite, it's not, it's deep, deep, deep): *You don't have to know or have all the answers. Trust in the One who does have them.* This is where the *rest* of God comes from. He says, "Be still and know that I am God." Live in an assured expectation of the appearance of His providence in your circumstances.

I don't know how my son is going to turn out—how his teenage years will look. Right now, from a natural point of view, it's 50/50, but I trust in the Supernatural One who knows all that. I have no idea where tomorrow's rent will come from, but I trust in the One who does. God says, "Read My lips and believe! Chillax!"[20]

Now here is a heavy.

If you do not have conviction that the same power that raised Christ from the dead lives in you and can transform your heart, family, and the world—it could have transformed Michael Jackson had he been willing—and that it will some-day transform your earthly body, then your faith is, for all intent, merely "religion." And according to the apostle Paul's letter to the first Christians, it is "worthless" to you and to your child, whom you should be raising with an eye toward that same conviction.[21] "Religion" robs us of power and victory. It also robs our children of power and victory. It robs the Lord of the glory due Him. Deep, huh? Avoid religion. Single Moms and Dads, we need all the power and victory we can get, and God deserves to be glorified. Rest well and know that God *will* be exalted and *will* work for His great name.

Say No to the Status Quo: Don't become so well-adjusted to the single-parent culture that you fit into it, into the stats, outcomes, methods, and expected results without even think-ing. Instead, fix your attention on God. You'll be changed from the inside out.[22]

Love as Fuel

God's gift of resurrection power is fueled by the love of the Father for humanity. It is like receiving a personal jet pack (think "The Jetsons") fueled by the limitless power of uncondi-tional love, sacrificial love (the blood of Jesus), the Living Word (Jesus), the Holy Spirit, grace, mercy, and forgiveness. It is the power of Love—who God is, who the Holy Spirit is, and who Jesus Christ is. Realize the depth of this…we have an infinite supply of love power available to us.

Are you ready to soar above social stigma? Are you ready to radically parent your child or children? How do you become radical? By getting radically real with God and believing that death and decay have no hold on your family. The only limit is the limit of your faith to receive it. Your parenting effective-ness will grow as your faith grows. Faith grows by knowing God through His Word, worship, and prayer. These are your lifelines to God.

What is faith? The substance of hope, a seed of infinite po-tential holding all possibilities within it. It is the foundation of our hope, and the conviction of things not seen. (See Hebrews 11:1.)

I know time is scarce and your days are busy, but you need to take time for God. Notice I said "take time," not "make time." Only God can make time. It is impossible to get every-thing done under our own steam! We need to know more about the power available to us on our journey and how it makes all things *realistically* possible, with time left over to enjoy God, enjoy our children, ~~play golf, visit friends, go to the spa,~~ and breathe!

> **Alert:** It's all in the Bible—God's Guide for Raising Children. I'm just posing as a highlighter, marking the points that worked for me and my son. By the way, keep the Word by your side as you read this book. Better yet, prioritize devotions and spend more time in the Bible than you do in this book or any other book. Faith comes by hearing the perfect Word of God, not by anything I tell you. The Bible is the best way to discern truth. Study the source so you can spot my inconsistencies. Moreover, the Father may just highlight something to you that will speak to your heart better than I ever can. Test everything here, and anything you read concerning parenting, according to the Word. Although I'm not perfect, God's Word is perfect. God is the Perfect Parent. What He says, believe. His Word settles everything.

Just How Much Power Do You Need?

The power available to you, dear single parent, is the same power that raised Jesus from the dead—the same power that brought my son to Christ, the same power that created for me a stay-at-home career, and the same power that has delivered me safely through the past six years alone. If He can do it for me, He can do it for you. If He could raise Christ, He can raise you and your child. Whoosh—now *that* is power! It is enough power to fill the void left by a missing parent or spouse, and enough power to transform not only your family, but every member of every family on the planet. There is power enough to transform, heal, and save everyone—a wayward child, a deadbeat dad, a wandering wife, Britney Spears—everywhere, every time, and every place. There is even power enough to save you from yourself. That's good, because we single moms and dads are just too hard on ourselves.

There is enough power to bring millions and billions to the knowledge of salvation and to bring nations to their knees. Jesus wants to use you and your family to do all this for His glory over the powers of darkness. For now, He wants you to concentrate on Him and your kids. I heard that sigh—like you want to be taking care of nations when it is all you can do to take care of your family! The "saving the nation task" is extreme, but not an impossibility in the presence of such power. Nevertheless, if you need time for yourself or extra time for a sick relative or to pull an extra shift, you'll need that kind of power applied to raising your little nation, because *God's power speeds up and eases the training process*. Read on. It's time to stop pulling out your hair!

- *His power draws your child because it is greater than any influence of media, peer pressure, drugs, alcohol, pornography, or lewdness, and more powerful than every temptation.*

- *Your child will not want to borrow power from the world, because he will have found all he needs, more than enough whenever he needs it from our triumphant, risen Christ. (See Eph. 3:20-21.)*

- *His power removes obstacles in the way or uses obstacles for the good and the glory of God.*

- *His power enables and empowers your child to endure under hardship and harsh conditions in obedience, faithfulness, self-control, kindness, and love.*

- *His power powers up your words and actions for astonishing results.*

Time Saver Alert: One minute of resurrection faith may be just as effective as an hour of prayer.

Believe for the Best

Whenever the worst happens, we and our children can know that the very best is near. As surely as our fingers are part of our hands, and our feet are part of our legs, so we are part of Christ's body, linked to Him as closely as body parts are connected. He is the Vine, and we are the branches. If we abide in Him and He abides in us, we will abundantly produce. If we live in Him and His words stay part of us, we can ask what we will, and it will be done for us. He, as a result, is glorified in our bearing much fruit as His disciples.[23]

We will share in the glory with Him because nothing can separate us from Him. We're stuck like glue. Grafted. No man, no woman, and no world can tear us apart. It is all on Christ's shoulders. Therefore, when something bad happens, we don't have to fall to pieces, fear death or sickness, fear the flu, terrorism, or world war, or even fear for the lives of our children. First, we know that Christ has been through it—the loss, pain, suffering, injustice, and temptation; and second, that it is just a passing thing, not our real life.

If Christ had not been raised, our hopes would be limited to this life, but because He was raised and lives in us, and, prayerfully, one day in our children as they make the choice to receive Him, the single-parent family—even with its disadvantages—can expect greater and greater things, can go from glory to glory to glory, rising to the task, maximizing and engaging the "dyna-might" power of God by faith.

And this is the way it has to be, Mom and Dad. Our children simply will not cope without hope. Nor can we. We can and must create and foster for our children an atmosphere of resurrection hope in our homes, because with hope comes "it has to happen" power to get through our single parenting and our single-parented child's challenges. Believing in the loving power of God is the key to maintaining parental poise (as opposed to curled up into the fetal position)!

Experience Problems Without Fear

If your child is to know Jesus and hide himself in Him, relying on the power of the Holy Spirit to get through what he has to get through in coming days, *you* will have to know Jesus and experience His love and His power. Do you have a personal knowledge and assurance of salvation? I invite you now to know the Lord Jesus Christ as your personal Savior who will send a Powerhouse life-giving Force (the Holy Spirit) to you, to help you raise your child with power, and lead him to that Power, for the glory of the Lord.

Lord Jesus, I want to know You personally, to have the assurance of living forever with You and my loved ones in eternity. Thank You for dying on the Cross for my sins to defeat death. I open the door of my life to You and ask You to come in as my Savior and the Lord of my life. Take control of it all. I surrender it to You. I give You my children and dedicate their lives to You, as I dedicate my life to the pursuit of righteousness for Your name's sake. Thank You for forgiving my sins, and giving me eternal life. Make me into the person You want me to be, and make us into a family determined to glorify You in all things. Amen!

Do you know that a heavenly host is cheering you on? They aren't your only fans. If you have given your life to Christ as a result of this book, please write and share your testimony—I'd like to celebrate with you and pray for you. You can find my contact information at the end of this book.

The Force Is With You

No, you are not hiding out, cowering behind the sofa playing peek-a-boo with the devil. Being hidden in Christ means that you have accepted Jesus, and He is the Way, Truth, Life, and Light of your life! You know and believe that Jesus died for humankind's sins, but what is more important, that He rose from death proving to all humanity (and your kids) that the Father grants the same eternal life to those who believe.

What lifted Jesus from death and the grave is not a what but a Who—the Force, the Powerhouse who is the Holy Spirit from God, the same Spirit given to all who profess and believe in Jesus. You now have that resurrection power in you and will know the mightiness of the risen Christ who is the Living Word beyond outward observation or surface knowledge.

As a believing single parent with your life hidden now with Christ in God, you can set your aim and sights high—as high as Heaven where Christ is seated at God's right hand for you and your kids. In Him, you are a force to be reckoned with in this world gone wild.

The Power Pack Advantage

The resurrection package is God's love gift to humanity, especially, I'm convinced, for solo parents. How vital to know that the moment you pray, the heavens are opened. With that kind of positive expectation set for your child, you will have a positive predictor of her ultimate outcome. You will believe in your child—*your* words, mannerism, actions, and thoughts will all reflect confidence in her abilities, gifting, talents, character, and self-esteem—and her sense of worth in the eyes of God will increase. If you believe in her as a conqueror, she will have the power to believe in herself too, giving her a self-assurance that is vital to everything she will do for the rest of her life.

If you are born again into God's family, I want you to know that this divine revelation of confidence in Christ was part of the package. It is within you, and it doesn't depend upon feelings. The love gift is in you—alive, vital, powerful, mighty, and more than enough to help you through your single-parent journey. Watch the stats soar with fresh favor over our single-parented children. The world will stand amazed at what Christ has accomplished through them.[24] Fly, baby, fly!

Pray

Father in Heaven, I pray that out of Your glorious riches You will strengthen me with power through Your Spirit in my inner being, so that You will dwell in my heart through faith. I pray that I am rooted and established in love, and can grasp how powerful, wide, long, high, and deep Your love really is. I pray to know Jesus and His love better and to be filled to the measure of all the fullness of God. Now to You—who is able to do immeasurably more than I ask or imagine, according to Your power that is at work within me—to You be glory in the Church throughout all generations, forever and ever! Amen. (See Eph. 3:16-21.)

Now, pray the same prayer again, inserting the names of each of your children at appropriate spots.

PART II

Activating Your Presence

CHAPTER 3

Busy Parent, Lonely Kids—*The Love Plan*

Remember, people will judge you by your actions, not your intentions. You may have a heart of gold—but so does a hardboiled egg.—Author Unknown

I f we cannot find time to hug, nurture, encourage, talk to, make eye contact with, and develop open relationships with our children, the results may cause tremendous damage—alienation, indifference, and too-early independence. While we do not mean to emotionally neglect our children, sometimes we do unintentionally shut them out.

Cultivating the "We" Plan

Sometimes I am so overwhelmed or preoccupied that I cut corners when it comes to spending time with DS. Even with a few spare moments, sometimes I'm too weary to interact constructively with him. I am guilty as charged for using the television or the computer as a surrogate parent. And it goes the other way too, when DS is involved in activities or with friends. We all get caught up in our own little worlds, and wonder why our families lack real identity. This is the problem today: "me" culture families rather than the "we" makeup of a healthy family.

If we are all caught up in our own little worlds, then it stands to reason that each of us stands alone. This is not a good atmosphere for fostering bonding love or interdependence. As a result, our children might turn to outside influences, which may not reflect our values.

Do you know who spends the most time influencing your child? How many hours per month does he spend on the Internet, playing video games, texting on a cell phone, listening to an iPod, reading magazines, or watching videos or television? Of all these outside sources of influence, how many possess the same values, beliefs, and standards that you have or expect for your child? The weaker their negative influence now, the greater the likelihood that your child will adhere to your values as she enters puberty and beyond. The more memories she has of mutual acceptance, trust, and loyalty between the parent and family members...the more time spent together living values and standards, the greater the anchor to yours.

Maximizing Together Time

It is difficult for us, as sole bread winners who wear all the hats, to find family together time. Therefore, it is essential for us to capitalize on what we do have, by sending the right messages when we *are* together, and maximizing the time we spend as a family. Feeling stretched? Even without enough time, rest assured, you have every reason to realistically believe in a solid, secure, functional, cohesive, interdependent, blessed, healthy, and *whole* family, with children who will soar and excel as lovers of the truth out there living it—even with the certainty that you will not do everything perfectly. How? Love is key; love covers imperfection. Your love itself greatly influences your child.

What You Can Do Now: Use family speak: "Wow, what an awesome family we are! I *love* this family."

Special Needs

Every child has special needs, but even more so for the child growing up in a single-parent family. More than our immediate physical needs, my son had to deal with fear, threats to his security, low self-esteem, feeling juggled and torn apart, having to adapt to two very different parenting approaches, and one extremely angry parent. As equally as important as *"For I was hungry and you fed me…naked and you clothed me…"* (Matt. 25:35) is: "You raised a standard. You grounded me. You sought to understand me. You told me I was OK. You modeled what I was to do. You made time. You comforted me. You loved me. You forgave me. You corrected me. You set me right. You looked me in the eye. You sought me out. You were always glad to see me!"

Fill Your Love Reservoir

I know what it is to grow up in a dysfunctional family. My father was a mean alcoholic. My mother, bless her heart, had a hard time of it with seven children who were all born within nine years of each other, an abusive spouse, and the hardships wrought by alcohol-acquired poverty. She'd often be sent to the hospital to rest, suffering depression and nervous breakdowns. I've always suspected, though, that part of her illness was due to postpartum depression, which wasn't well-known or properly diagnosed and treated in the 1960s. In those days, they treated many such women, including my mother, with shock therapy and barbiturates—travesty!

When Mom was home, however, she aimed high and with the best standards in a substandard situation. Somehow, as weary and run down as she was, her love reservoir never ran out. I knew she loved and cherished me. She hugged and kissed a lot, spoke eye to eye with me, had a tender touch, and made me feel like a favorite child—in fact, she made all seven of us feel that way. She affirmed and encouraged, sang "You are my sunshine" to us, and, although she wept often, somehow she managed to smile through her tears, which conveyed a "no matter what, I will always love you" message.

By and by, Dad left my mother for another woman with three children. Mom just could not manage alone, and she had to "let us go," although she hung on way past her breaking point. We became wards of the court and entered the foster care system to live with strangers. Her love clung to me, and I never once felt rejected. I carried every confidence that, even apart, I would always be in her heart. I carried her love inside my suitcase! But my father's love, not so much. Sober or drunk, he ruled dictator-style when he was around, and over and over again he sent us a message of desertion. Tucked inside a pocket of my heart was a wee fear and mistrust of father figures, but love fixed that, when at the age of 13, I came to know the

Father in Heaven through His Son Jesus who became my personal Lord and Savior.

Love Births Character

I've surmised that the tenacity of my mother's love communicated a message of value. That security miraculously birthed vital and core character traits and values uncharacteristic of children from abusive homes. My first foster mother, Mother B, who is still very much part of my life, shared with me that the day my 10-year-old twin brother and I arrived at her home, she was expecting ruffians. But to her surprise, we surpassed even her own children when they were our age, in emotional maturity, well-being, and security, and in politeness, kindness, and composure.

The Lord, in His mercy and grace, and in answer to a praying aunt's pleas for our family, preserved my mother's ability to love and communicate love tenderly in a hard setting. As a result, love preserved *me*, shielded me, protected me, and manifested positive attributes—I am confident of this! It must have been a miracle, for few women could have endured the hardships my mother did without becoming hardened, mean, resentful, or bitter. Not once do I ever remember an unkind word from her. Despite our difficulties, few such children turn out as right as we did.

Did my mother teach or model all the things I needed to know as a youngster? No. Did she provide me with everything I needed? No. Was she perfect?

She was perfect *enough*.

Perfect in love. Because love covered all lack, real and perceived. Yes, I had issues to work through, and yes, some things my father did (abuse, neglect) scarred all of us somewhat, but I could constantly apply the balm of the love I knew from my mother, even in the short time we had together. When my self-esteem was tested, because of this knowledge of my true self-worth, I was able to stand firm. Eventually I was able to heal and trust in the love of surrogate parents.

Today as a parent, I take the very best that Mom had, that perfect thing she did right, and model it for my son. The feeling of being loved. What a legacy!

What You Can Do Now: If love is all you have, give it all you've got! And be spontaneous with it!

How Secure Do You Feel?

Tom noted when his 4-year-old daughter exhibited symptoms of insecurity shortly after he and his wife's separation. "Missy moped around the house with a long face and nothing I did could shake her out of it. One day I realized my little girl was mirroring me. She needed a building block upon which to step up, but I had become her stumbling block."

Jesus says that people will observe the light we shine in our life.[25] We can tell our children all day long how God feels about them, how we feel about them, what they are supposed to do, how they are supposed to act, but the truth is they will emulate us. As they mature, they will model their lives after what they experience. Our emotions, lifestyle, character, and choices are all in a figurative picture frame they will hopefully display and pass on to the family for generations. We leave a legacy, good or bad—we must choose good, or else we'll end up in someone's attic for a dusty future!

Your mistakes may feel permanent, but God is masterfully redemptive! Go ahead, tell Him that you want to be whole so your family can be whole. Ask Him to bring about His very best, even if things don't look so good right now.

What You Can Do Now: Check yourself—Are you a positive role model? One less person affirming, teaching, equipping, and positively leading a child increases the risk of major insecurities, as do single parents with low self-worth. Parents feeling insecure about themselves can pass their feelings on to a child. Kids can feel it when their parents have lost hope. Gotta love the (former) Home Depot motto, "To improve everything we touch." Are we improving our children?

Power Up: So far, so God! It's always good to have an open-door policy for God. He shouldn't have to knock all the time!

Love Flows Through Flaws

Perfect love empowers us to view our mistakes, flaws, and regrets as valuable parenting tools and self-help nuggets. If I snap at DS without thinking…bingo, an opportunity to model repentance and humility presents itself. By and by, DS stops using it as leverage to get what he wants and says, "It's OK, Mom, I forgive you!" Who knew the snap of one elastic band could reap such marvelous reward? I snap. He learns. Priceless!

Today he usually forgives and apologizes without prompting. And my patience has improved a hundredfold. Your positive actions now can make your child want to hang out with you and tell you his secrets. Guess what? If your child sees you shape your worries into prayers, she may do the same![26]

Consider...

What does your child see when your spousal support or child support check is two months late and the telephone is about to be cut off? Do you panic? Or do you boost up your confidence in God?

What does your child see when you don't think you can handle one more crisis? Does he see a great big God as you fall on your knees, or a God too small to handle your situation as you crumble to the floor?

What does your child see when you are afraid of an uncertain outcome? Hopefully, she sees you releasing your fears to God, inviting His presence in the situation.

Get a Divine Handle on Things

The way you handle the difficult circumstances ultimately determines what your child believes about God and His promises. If you wait upon God to renew your strength, your child will see you soar up with wings like eagles. She will marvel at the way a geriatric like you can run and not be weary, or walk, and not faint! (See Isa. 40:31.)

On the other hand, if you are not friendly to yourself, or are unrealistic about your abilities and limitations, your child will have a harder time.

Communicate: I Love You

Showing love through relationship with God and with each other is vital. Relationship with God early in life is a child's best opportunity to overcome the obstacles that come his way. The next most important ingredient in helping your child handle peer pressure, transitions, negative influences, the flesh, and crises, is a vital, contagious, loving relationship with *you*.

"I love you," are three words that your child needs to hear from you. She needs to *see* love too, with a look, a smile, a touch, a thoughtful gesture, and tenderness. This requires your *active presence*. Lovingly and freely invest as much of your active presence as you can with your family. Communicate love through action and interaction, words and deeds, with caring, patient character, by making the most of your time together every day. How you convey your love in words and actions will define forever how she sees or views Mom or Dad, and perhaps even affect the way in which she views God the Father. She will always remember how you were and what you did. What do your actions tell your child? Yikes, four years ago, my own actions would have said, "Messed up!"

Dads Raising Girls

A single, widowed father friend raising four children on his own—with one daughter in a college nursing program and "a good girl"—credits his success to the following:

- *Keeping communication open, especially in her teen years. Really listening to what is going on in her life rather than overreacting by immediately running toward a solution, like "grabbing for the gun!"*

- *Being her father, not her friend or her mother! Being her "gentle" man—treating her gently like a princess, by opening doors, avoiding rough play, and nurturing in a fatherly way.*

- *Respecting women, never degrading them, and always avoiding sexist remarks.*

- *Never teasing her about her looks. Reinforcing how beautiful she is to me, especially commenting on her inward loveliness and assets.*

- *Keeping a good number of godly, strong, capable, and motherly female mentors in her life: aunts, grandmother, a close family friend who is also a mother. They have really helped me with the more sensitive issues, such as puberty and dating!*

- *Being involved in her life. As hard as it was for me to juggle work and household stuff, I did all I could to be present—I was around when her friends visited, at soccer practices and games, and at school events.*

- *Finding common interests. We loved to walk and explore nature, and collected stuff we found along the way for a basket we had at home. We also loved garage sales.*

- *Avoiding the trap of letting her become mother to myself and to my boys!*

- *Helping her feel safe confiding in me. Realizing that what seemed big to her may appear small to me. At first, I tried to minimize her feelings, but later, a female friend showed me that I should seek to understand what the situation means to my daughter, rather than to myself.*

- *Showing her how confident I was about our future as a family and her future, and modeling trust in God for wonderful outcomes by dealing with problems head-on, first, through prayer.*

- *Giving her privacy. And ensuring that the boys gave it to her as well.*

- *Developing house rules concerning appropriate dress.*

- *I had to be careful not to "over-princess" her, in that when she was eight she was convinced that she could do no wrong! I hated to knock her off that pedestal, but actually, when I followed through with consequences, it set her higher, because afterward she realized just how unconditional my love for her was.*

Moms Raising Boys

Boys have a hero thing going on, a need to be brave and daring, but that shouldn't be a problem in a single-mother household. Use it to your advantage! Ridding the house of spiders comes to mind! DS, as all boys do, needs adventure and challenge, and most boys enjoy physical activity, although that is changing due to computers and video gaming. It is still important to get boys outdoors and active, and it helps to seek out a few reliable, trustworthy, godly male role models and mentors to help out. When my son was in baseball, it truly helped encourage team spirit, values, perseverance, and yes, even strength of character.

It also helps to establish a common ground with your son. I do this with DS by finding things we both like that can stimulate conversation and fun! When he was young, we started collecting stamps, shells, and rocks, which still keep us busy, rain or shine. I draw the line at anything to do with snakes or spiders, however. Eek! Together, as time permits, try to get out and do typically "male" things; for instance, check out that high rise building being built down the street, go tadpole hunting, or visit ~~the Harley dealership~~ a car show.

Here are some other things that have helped me raise DS into manhood. I'm including some tips from Jeanie, a friend and a single divorced mother of a daughter and son. Hers was a bitter divorce. Thankfully she saw the error of her ways, and grew wiser as a result!

- *As tough as it might be, respect your son's father and support their relationship. Never, ever compare your son to his father unless it is in a positive light.*

- *Avoid losing your leverage by over-negotiating with your son. Less said is always better in the long run.*

- *Read up on hormones. Specifically testosterone, and how it affects your son's behavior and thought patterns. Discover what to do about it, and quickly, even before he turns 12!*

- *Be his mother, not his friend. Conversely, don't let him father you, befriend you, or take over your house! Treat him as a child who will grow into manhood.*

- *Keep structure, consistency, and order in your lives. (This brought Heather's son around from acting out in anger because of the confusing melting pot of emotions he was going through.)*

- *Capitalize on teachable moments. Point out good men who reflect high standards and great moral character, such as godly actors, teachers, or sports figures. Tell your son their stories, or better yet, provide some first-hand accounts.*

- *Be tolerant and respectful of your son's uniquely male traits—they are God-ingrained. And whatever you do, never, ever crush his spirit.*

The lists above comprise just a few good parenting tips for single moms and dads. Please check out the resource list in the back of this book for further study.

Role Models

Everyone you bring into your child's life is a role model, good or bad. Do you know the morals and values of uncles, aunts, cousins, friends, babysitters, and the impact their positive or negative values will have? Your son or daughter is better off without a role model than with a wrong one. Be careful. You might have many volunteers, but only a few will do. Only allow in the few in whom you completely trust. I would venture, if you have any doubt at all, to do a thorough check.

Also watch out that you don't find someone who promises your child the world, and does not deliver. Unreliability or reneging on promises can be devastating, and does not set a good example. If you are a dad and dating, ask yourself, "Do I want my daughter to be like her?" If you are a mom and dating, would you want your son to be like him? Or like any of the people who spend much time with you?

Fill the Family Love Tank

Here are some great ideas that worked for me with DS:

Hug him until he lets you go.

Tell him "God loves you" often.

Pray, worship, and read the Bible together.

Ask him to teach you something.

Learn his opinions and views on different subjects.

Sing and laugh often.

Learn his lingo and body language.

Read First Corinthians 13 together.

Record and watch a program together that you both enjoy.

Play hide and seek indoors for a change.

Place notes in his lunchbox, under his pillow, on the bathroom mirror.

Build things together, or take them apart.

Display his artwork and assignments all over the house.

Show an interest in his friends.

Record a love message for him when you are away.

Get a bearded dragon (DS made me throw that one in).

Know Your Child's Receptors

Each child expresses and receives love in unique and preferred ways, which can change as they mature. However, please note that if verbalizing "I love you" is not something you feel comfortable with, other attempts to relay the message may fail. Your child needs to hear it from your lips in good times, and in not so good times.

The first step is to discover the most effective way to express your love. It may not be the way in which you love to be loved. As a little guy, DS enjoyed the feeling of touch: hugs, kisses, cuddling, close play, wiping back a wisp of hair, his face held in my hands. Some children prefer however, to hear about your love more than they want the physical closeness. Others want to see expressions through visual means, like loving notes tucked inside a lunch box, a gesture, or eye-to-eye contact. Some kids desire you to be nearby always, while others want their space. DS? He wants both! "Mom, I need you." "Leave me alone!"

We get so busy, we forget to convey our love beyond the mundane chores and meeting their daily needs. Some parents I know (particularly fathers), never tell their children "I love you." But I think saying, "I love you," at least six times a day is not optional. Plan also to purposely convey your love to each child individually in other ways daily, and to the family as a unit, perhaps with a game, outing, craft project, or treasure hunt at least once a week! Stay with your love plan, observe changes, and rejoice!

As you begin to consistently lavish your child with your love, he will come to that place of trust, response, security, and rest in your unconditional warmth and affection, the best behavior therapy around! Let go of any worries that you will spoil your child or make him too dependent upon you. Loving DS actually *released* him toward healthy independence.

What if They Reject Our Love?

It is important that we love our kids extravagantly. But what happens when they face rejection outside of the home—when they encounter a world that does not love them as we do?

As much as we love them unconditionally, the world will not. Can they handle it? In Chapter 7 I tackle the problem of low self-esteem, and how to recognize it, root it out, and significantly help children become accountable for it because self-esteem is something we cannot ultimately give them. With high, godly self-esteem our children will gain confidence in the power of God in their lives to rise above negative influences and losses, something that threatens youth in particular today.

CHAPTER 4

"Help! I've Got An Owie I Can't Fix!"—*Nurture Your Child Through Loss and Transition*

Perhaps the greatest social service that can be rendered by anybody to this country and to mankind is to bring up a family.—George Bernard Shaw

Separation and divorce is stressful for children; and although reactions vary depending on a child's age, predisposition, and the circumstances, it is not uncommon for some children to act out because of what is going on inside, or to blame you alone for the circumstances.

Although Keith (not his real name), tried to convince his 10-year-old son to the contrary, his son still feels somewhat to blame for the divorce. "Mike spends much more time in his room now, and responds in anger to even simple requests." Although it has been over a year and he is seeing some improvement in his son, there is growing resentment. Keith wonders,

"When will this adjustment come, or does it ever come, and how can I facilitate my son's healing?"

DS also went through this, and from time to time, resentment still rears. I helped him successfully transition by minimizing the tension, being patient while he adjusted, encouraging communication, and responding openly and honestly to his concerns.

Getting Personal Things in Order Quickly

Here are some other things that worked for me. First, I maintained a civil relationship with DS's father. Prior conflict between us caused DS tremendous stress and angst, so resolution was something I needed to prioritize, otherwise, this confluence of anger may have carried into his adulthood. Although occasional arguments are normal in a family, for a child constantly in the middle of a battleground, it is a huge burden. If either parent cannot come to resolution, I would suggest seeking help from a pastor, counselor, or mediator, to help sort out problems, arrive at solutions, and come to a place of forgiveness, so that you can all move toward emotional health and well-being.

Once you are able to maintain a good relationship with an ex-spouse, bring that other parent into the deeper conversations you are having with your child concerning the breakup—and be sure to leave blame, anger, and bitterness out of it. Tailor the talk to your child's age and maturity level. I recall when DS, age 9, asked us both if we could get back together. This is one example of a deeper talk you might be able to have with your child, once you and your ex-spouse are on better terms. Of course, the primary message you want to convey to your child is, "It's not your fault! You are not to blame for Dad and me splitting up." This might take ongoing reassurance, as it did for DS.

DS had to know that it was OK for him to be upset and sad. I did not want him to worry that my love for him would run out, that I would abandon him as a result, or that his sadness added to my burdens or those of his father's. It took some doing, but both his dad and I learned how to hear his heart, to perceive his fears, and to help allay them.

If you and your ex can get to the place of "We love you so much and are sorry about our breakup and how it is hurting you. What can we do to help you through this?" you have climbed Everest and are well on your way toward helping your child heal. Understand that your child's fears are very real. DS had fears of abandonment, fears that I would get sick and die, "…and then what will happen to me?"

Equipping for Change

While we were in the throes of change, it helped DS immensely when I equipped and prepared him for those changes. I answered every question he had about how his life would change as honestly as I could and within my power to predict, so he could understand the process and think through it. For an 8-year-old little guy, oh my, that was tough!

But I also wanted him to know that his feelings and opinions mattered. For instance, a big fear was about changing schools, which meant leaving his friends and fearing he would not be accepted in the new school. Once I knew his fear, I could deal with it and work together with his father to ensure we did all that we could to keep him in his school. And we did!

It really helped to keep at least one constant in his life, and this constant spring-boarded his adjustment to other changes.

For the things that must change, be honest and reassure your family that you will all get through it, even though it may take time. Your child does not need the details, although she might ask for them, so use your judgment and simplify, especially when your child is young. Older children and teens tend to be more in tune with what you have been going through and may ask deeper questions depending on what they have already picked up from you, know to be true, or have heard.

Talks about divorce or separation should be ongoing, because as children grow, they process different chunks of it, and some of those chunks breed more chunks. It is amazing that after six years, DS still asks questions, though they are framed differently, and he requires deeper answers. The more he ponders, the more questions he hadn't thought of before, like, "Did you love Daddy when you had me?"

Some questions I still haven't answered to DS's satisfaction, yet he still asks. Either I haven't been sufficient with my answers, or the topic goes far below the surface. Time might reveal, but in the meantime, I pray for all of his hurts to disappear, his doubts to vanish; and I keep an eye on how those unanswered questions affect his morale and emotional health, in case he needs additional help beyond what I can give.

Observing your child may clue you in to how she is feeling. Bobbie's daughter, after his divorce, tried to over-please him, and constantly put on the "happy-happy," a cover-up to help her avoid coming to terms with the breakup of her family. DS too for a time covered up what he was feeling by putting on a brave front. However even though he seemed emotionally healthy, I constantly reassured in words and in actions, while encouraging him to open up and share what he was feeling. It is vital that he knows how important his feelings are to both parents, and that his feelings will be taken seriously.

In DS's case, he simply could not describe his feelings, but at times I found it helped to get it started by asking probing questions: "You seem sad…Do you know why?" Sometimes what he shared was difficult to hear, even hurtful, and I was tempted to close the conversation, but so grateful I did not, because dumping on me made him feel a whole lot lighter. Me, not so much!

After I was sure he'd gotten it all out, and only when I understood where he was coming from, did I offer appropriate support, solutions, and ways to make things better, thereby validating his feelings. "I miss my old neighborhood, my friends, Mom," he finally blurted out one day.

"You're right, it does feel quiet around here…it is lonely without our friends, isn't it? What do you think will help you get over missing your friends?" He suggested that I call one of his friend's mothers, and invite the family over for dinner. This empowered him! If your child does not discover a solution, suggest a few things like, "Why don't we drive through the old neighborhood."

Our divorce was devastating to DS—a true and significant loss of the kind of life he once had. And because for a time I was mourning, until I rose from my ash heap, he suffered double. As with an actual death, in divorce your children are potentially in mourning, and grief is a process that takes time. According to Mandy, whose husband left suddenly for another woman, the real impact can be felt for as long as two or three years.

"We were all in shock, and getting to the next level took a few months. We could not move on until we could process the fact that he wasn't coming back. It has been two years now, and we are all just coming to a place of healing and understanding," she said. Eventually, everyone in the family accepts the new situation. If time doesn't help heal, consider pastoral counseling.

What Helped Pull Both of Us Out!

The following are things I did that helped pull DS and me out of the I-can't-believe-this-happened funk:

- *Developed consistency and routine.*

- *Resisted the urge to spoil him.*

- *Lavished him with love.*

- *Had one-on-one time with him regularly—quick trips, walks, nature trails.*

- *Sought help when some strange behavior and minor depression emerged, before it became a pattern.*

- *Gave him time to adjust and to grieve.*

- *Sought help from our pastor, his teacher, and a school counselor.*

- *Gave him time with friends who had been through similar situations.*

- *Stayed physically, emotionally, and spiritually healthy.*

- *Took the high road with his father; put away blame, vengefulness, bitterness, snarkiness, put downs, and negativity.*

- *Determined not to use DS or depend on him to report the carryings on of his father, nor did I use him as a pawn to get what I wanted from his father, nor did I use him as a messenger. "Tell your dad…" is so wrong!*

Death and Transition

Jesus says, *"I am telling you the truth: You will cry and be sad, but the people of the world will be glad. You will be full of sorrow, but your sorrow will change into joy."*[27]

If a parent or a loved one dies, just as with divorce it is sometimes difficult to know how to help the child cope with the loss, particularly as you work through your own grief and personal upheaval. Philip's wife died two years ago, and it has been especially hard on his 10-year-old boy. "He's sad all the time, looks out into space, and has become more withdrawn than the other children."

How much your child can understand about death depends on his age, beliefs, life experiences, and tendencies. Recovery takes time, more time for some children than others. It is like a series of waves, according to my widow and widower friends, and in my own experience as a teen of losing my birth mother in a fire, I hid my grief behind a wave. Some children hold back their grief so that they won't make you sadder or cause you more worry. I know that I felt cheated out of my time with Mom, and didn't want to get over the loss because in some strange way it kept her present. In more extreme cases, a child might feel he or she cannot go on. In this case, immediate professional intervention is necessary. Here are some things many of us have found that have helped our children:

What You Can Do Now:

1. Be honest with your child and encourage questions, even if you don't have the answer to "Why did Daddy leave me?"

2. Create an atmosphere of openness and safety when communicating, whether in anger or sadness.

3. Don't be afraid to let your child see you cry, but also model that life does go on.

4. Explain things in an age-appropriate way.

    At age 5, DS took things quite literally so when his Uncle Ho-Jo died, I avoided telling him things like "Uncle Ho-Jo has gone to sleep" or "We have lost him." I remember as a child being told this after an aunt died and actually becoming afraid to go to bed at night for fear I would never awaken. Also avoid saying things like, "You've lost your daddy," because it might make your child fearful of your getting lost and never coming home. I found that DS understood concrete things much better. It helped to find a picture Bible to help explain death and the afterlife.

    Thankfully, I did lead his uncle to the Lord while on his deathbed, so I could actually show DS through pictures of Heaven and of Jesus' resurrection from the dead, the good news about loving Jesus and the hope of one day seeing our loved ones again in Heaven, the place God calls our home.

    If your spouse was not a believer, while you have no definitive way of knowing if he or she made it to heaven, you can be assured and can assure your child that God's utmost desire was for him or her to be with Him forever. (God's desire is that not one person is lost!) Thus it would make sense that God by His Spirit would do His utmost, until the last breath or who knows, to woo the loved one unto Himself.

For certain you can say something like, "God loves your mommy so much, I'm sure He invited her to Heaven." At around age 7, DS could better grasp the finality of death but until our precious Black Labrador Retriever, Cash, died, did not believe it would happen in our household, given that he had prayed that God would "deliver us from evil," and keep everyone alive forever and ever.

At that time, DS was 8. It would have been a disservice to him not to deal with Cash's death simply and truthfully, with clear explanations about how Cash died.

Some of us may try to personify death; that is, to say that the loved one has become an angel or a ghost, but this is unbiblical and untrue.

It just does not happen, and death ultimately becomes scarier and confusing to the child in the long run.

Now that DS is a teen, he questions mortality and his own vulnerability more frequently, although at times he acts as if he is invincible! The loss of my step-daughter's best friend launched the deeper question: "What is the meaning of life?" and brought on extreme lows and guilt. We need to be careful that our teens do not slip into depression.

5. Give your child breathing room. Peter, the widower, understood that his way of grieving the loss of his murdered wife was not his children's way of grieving for their mother. "I had to be patient with my youngest who acted out his grief, and with my oldest son who seemed angry all the time and pulled away from me. I gave Matt the space that he needed, and did not take Joshua's anger personally, overreact, nor did I isolate him. We all had our different process of recovery." Do watch for signs that your child needs your help or additional professional help. Radical changes beyond normal behavior especially require immediate help from a doctor, pastor, counselor, or grief specialist, along with intercessory prayer. If your child is grieving for a long time without feeling any better, if your child is depressed, if your child's grief is so intense she cannot concentrate in school or shuts out friends, if she cannot sleep, eat, or if she communicates a desire for death (What is Heaven like? Will I go to Heaven? Will I see my mother there?), hurts herself, or attempts suicide, get swift help through professional, spiritual, and emotional counseling.

6. *Reign in the help* of extended family members (grandparents, aunts, uncles) or close family friends. Encourage your child to talk about his feelings with them as well as with you.

Encouraging Ideas

- *Encourage your child to keep a memory journal about the parent who died, and about his feelings. Have him write a poem, song, or a tribute.*

- *Invite ongoing visits by friends and family so that your child does not feel isolated but feels reassured.*

- *Go for frequent walks and bicycle rides together in the fresh air. Something about God's nature gives us a sense of hope and renewal. It also gives your child exercise that helps motivate and alleviate a bad mood.*

- *Don't try to hide pictures of your spouse or remove all his or her possessions from the home right away. Dealing with your loved one's personal effects does not need to happen right away.*

- *Create a memorial or a tribute. Plant a tree or a garden, enter a charity run or a walk, design a Website, or create a memory table in the home with special photos and items that the parent loved.*

- *Encourage a return to life, extra-curricular activities, school, and friends. Going back to enjoying life does not mean your child no longer misses his father or mother.*

- *Each day does get easier. You can help lighten your child's days by bringing a smile to his face. Do his chores for a few days, read the Bible together, serve him dessert or a meal in bed, create a secret love reminder code, or do something out of the ordinary routine.*

Distance Separation

Extended business trips, military deployment, illness, or even a parent at home but not "at home" and participating (if you know what I mean) may create the feeling of a single-parent scenario in your home. Consider the parent living with a computer addict. There, but not there!

DS as a youngster had difficulty understanding that absent did not mean "gone forever," when I had to travel on business or visit an ailing family member. However, as he matured and grew to understand that I would be coming home, there were times he took advantage of one less rule enforcer present!

I believe all children feel the lack of involvement of the other parent in their lives with a "there, but not there" scenario—probably the worst in terms of a child not feeling loved by the parent who neglects him. Here are some things that have helped me and others with our children, and may help your child feel more secure.

- *Foster a sense of stability. Through the small things that stay the same, like mealtimes and bedtimes. These routines helped with DS's sense of security and well-being. Acknowledge feelings. Your child, as DS did, may feel angry or fearful. Again, understand where your child is coming from. Allow him to give voice to his feelings.*

- *Maintain a connection. My friend Judy's husband frequently traveled, sometimes for months. To help especially her younger children understand that their daddy had not abandoned them and would be coming home, they wrote letters and emails, and even video conferenced online to help strengthen their connection. A countdown calendar and a map pinpointing where in the world the parent is are two of many ways you can reassure your child. Connecting may not always be possible, especially if the parent is deployed but keeping a scrapbook and photos and reminders of the other parent around, and writing letters and sending care packages will help. In the case of the simply uninvolved parent, try unplugging the computer or the television.*

- *Stay healthy and emotionally stable. It is easy to become exhausted and overwhelmed by handling things on your own—bills, calls from the teacher, or transporting kids to activities. Goodness, how I know this! Enlist the support of your church, friends, neighbors, and family to help all of you through this time, particularly if you yourself find it hard to positively give attention to the children.*

CHAPTER 5

How to Open Soft-Shell Clams—
Even if Grounded for Life

A dead spirit is an incommunicative one. Teasing, name calling, and unkind words are as hard as cannonballs to a child, even with a "just kidding" thrown in with the lob. Names such as "Stupid" or "Dumb Ass" did terrible things to DS's heart and emotions, and bred an apathetic, rebellious, and closed spirit. The problem of teasing crushed him.

When I was a kid, people called me names, too, turning my maiden name, Manuel, into "Man, you smell!" Ouch!

As much as I've tried as a mother to encourage a male child, positive reinforcement from his father or a fatherly male role model will speed the process of healing and fill his heart with a sense of unconditional value and worth as a young man, and as a result, he will open up more. Of course, God has already done wonders—and thankfully, He has encouraged me to convey the message to DS that he is a precious gift!

Becoming Word Perfect

Parents need to be very careful with their words! Our children have such soft shells, and clam up when they are hurting or feeling insecure. Consider how God the Father praised Jesus. The writers of the New Testament thought it of great importance and included His exact words in each of their firsthand accounts: *"This is My beloved Son in whom I am well pleased!"* Jesus received honor and glory from His Father. (See Matt. 3:17, Mark 1:11, Luke 3:22, and 2 Peter 1:17.)

What You Can Do Now: Feed your child kind, uplifting, and complimentary *true* words. Be specific and sincere. "You showed so much courage when…" "I love the way you…" "I can depend on you because…" I never worry that DS will become prideful or stuck up; sincere, healthy words have helped build confidence, security, and have encouraged openness.

Positive words will work wonders coming from someone who knows your child best, and she likely won't hear it from other sources. And don't limit uplifting words to speech. Tuck a note in his lunch box, write a note on her computer screensaver, or without getting too personal, let her "overhear" you brag about her on the phone to the other parent, to a relative, or to a friend—this works!

Straight Talk: When I am maxed out in the tired aisle, I particularly need to watch my words. "Hurry up, Slowpoke" may seem harmless—but you never know what can manifest as a result—a two-toed sloth comes to mind!

Positive Names

Positive nicknames can be a super tool, although don't embarrass your child in front of peers. You'll know best whether to keep it private or not. Some nicknames I've used for DS: Wise King Sol, David the Giant Slayer, Beloved, Precious One, Apple of My Eye, and Warrior.

Power Up: Some children have a hard time accepting praise—but keep doing it. Persevere, and look for ways to bypass their built-up defenses. Don't stop—they will never outgrow their need for sincere praise.

R-e-s-p-e-c-t = Talk

Mary's son, Philip, has had a problem with feeling accepted, and it is something they continue to work on. As a youngster, Philip's dad was athletic, playing and excelling in many sports. As is true of many Dads, he expected his son would have a similar aptitude. They enrolled Philip into the local baseball league when he was about 7 years of age, and his father signed up as coach. The boy showed great promise as a pitcher, batted well enough, but had extreme difficulty as a runner.

Almost every game ended in disappointment for Philip, even if he did well, because he felt as if he couldn't live up to his father's expectations. "Why did you do this?…How come you did that?…If you did what I told you…." He was constantly told about the things he did wrong, and was pressured to be as good a baseball player as his father was at that age. As a result, it was a struggle to keep him motivated for the sport.

Mary recalls one important game when Philip was called up to the pitcher's mound. His father kept shouting orders to him from the sideline as he wound up for his pitches. He walked the first two batters. "You know better!" screamed his dad, arms flailing, rushing out to the mound.

"Dad, if you will just let me concentrate on the pitch and the batter, I can do it! I know what I need to do!" cried Philip, and he broke down right there in front of the crowd and his teammates.

His father pulled him by the arm off the field, all the while yelling at him, and made him sit out the rest of the game. For the rest of the season, Philip did not do very well. "Mom," he said, "I hate the game—I just can't please him."

Philip had the potential to be a great pitcher with the league, but because the coach, his dad, did not accept or respect his style (requiring concentration at the wind up), or respect his capabilities or opinions, he grew resentful and rebellious. By and by, Philip quit the game, and he also quit talking to his dad.

Assess: Is your child able to express her opinions and feelings even if they are not in line with yours? Do you listen to your child's point of view? It does not mean that you always must accept her decision, particularly if it compromises moral principles, values, conduct, or is harmful or has the potential to be—but do you understand where she is coming from? Or do you give her the silent treatment? Oh, that's a bad one! Do you dictate? Your child is always worthy of respect, even if she does do something wrong. Do you nit pick? Expect perfection? Compare her to other girls, to her brothers and sisters?

Perhaps you want your son to become a music prodigy but he wants to try out for the basketball team. How do you handle that? Sometimes we aim so high for our kids that when they can't achieve a standard, we make them feel like failures.

By the way, sometimes our own fears that our children will turn out wrong or be hurt in some way negatively influences our words or actions—drives us to drive them toward perfection. We don't really mean to cut our children down, and may not even be aware of our negativity, but it is a certain recipe for dead silence.

What You Can Do Now: Encourage and convey safety, security, and self-acceptance. Like you, your child is only being human. Respect that.

Respect + Talk = Acceptance

The "If I were you" approach is not a healthy one. My son is not me, and thank goodness for that! Unless he specifically asks, "Mom, what would you do?" I don't tell him. "What would Jesus do," is a much better approach. Our children will not have a lasting sense of high self-esteem unless their unique identity is hidden in Christ. Our job is to get them to believe that when God created them, He did not use a mold; each person has uniqueness, with qualities, talents, gifts, mannerisms, fingerprints, and footprints of their own. Encourage your child to discover her supernaturally beautiful uniqueness and to rely on the strengths of who she is in order to overcome fear, pass the tests, make the team, handle disappointment, and navigate through life.

Do you respect your child for who she is? We should treat our children with respect, from an attitude of humility.

Bitterness toward a spouse can create underlying resentments of a child who might remind you of your husband or wife. We must keep this in check for sure. We may expect our children to breeze through something that we breezed through, but while they are the fruit of our loins, they may not have the same makeup we have.

What You Can Do Now: Don't complain about your child or treat him as a burden; be grateful for him as a blessing from God. Don't offend or cause your child to stumble. Pray for the mind of Christ, asking to see your child as God sees him.

Straight Talk: Some of us live vicariously through our children, pushing them to achieve something we could not. This spells d-e-j-e-c-t-i-o-n and creates feelings of failure. Do we negatively put our children down for not being as good, smart, athletic, or well-behaved as we were? Do we value their unique abilities? Do we respect their dreams? Watch sentences like, "I can't believe you are afraid of spiders," or "I did, I can't see why you haven't been able to…"

Don't assume that you know what they are thinking, why they made a mistake, or that you know everything—most often, you will be wrong. Instead of saying, "I was your age once, you know," or "You should know better," I probe DS, "What are you going through? Is it difficult being the only boy in class wearing glasses? Do the kids tease you? How does that make you feel? I am sorry you are feeling left out."

Tugs of war increase as children seek and establish their own identity. This is still true of DS. My challenge is to let him gradually grow into himself while at the same time, keep communication doors and windows open as he navigates through the highs and lows of the process of discovery.

Reactions to Avoid

Here are some classics to avoid:

- *If only you acted more like your brother.*

- *Do you want to be grounded for life?*

- *End of discussion.*

- *Shut your mouth.*

- *Wipe that look off your face.*

- *Do you actually think you are…?*

- *As long as you live here, you will do exactly as I say.*

- *Do you understand me, young lady?*

- *Do you think I am made of money?*

- *Who do you think you are?*

Confidence = Talk

Your encouragement is key to your child's confidence in Christ, confidence in himself, and confidence in you. We simply cannot waver in the encouragement department. God tells us to encourage one another in Him. The message is clear throughout the Bible, "You are more than a conqueror in Christ." "You can do it because God says that He will never leave or forsake you!" "You can do it because God says 'You can do all things through Christ who gives you strength.'"[28] *"The grass withers and the flowers fall, but the word of our God stands forever."*[29] What He says is true. If your child learns to shift the focus from the problem onto Christ and His promises, he enters into a supernatural realm of doing the impossible. The message is,

"You can do it! You are strong, you are talented, you have common sense, you are wise, you are able to do this because God is on your side and ahead of you. I'm so glad you're my child!"

The last thing I thought my son would excel at is public speaking. Naturally shy, he usually tries to avoid notice. However, while in third grade, the entire school participated in a two-week public speaking program. Every child was required to speak in front of his or her class on a topic of choice. Classmates would vote on the top three oral presentations, and the winner from each class would speak in front of judges, parents, and the entire school. Runners-up would have the option of presenting and introducing each contender for the finals.

When DS pulled his assignment out of his backpack, he said, "Mom, I hate this—but if I win the class thing—no way will I go before the entire school." Ah, a spark of confidence, and did I detect desire? *"If* I win..."

I fanned it. "It's up to you, but I'm confident you can do it. Remember how well you did with show and tell in second grade? Remember how Moses was a stutterer, but God used him to lead a nation?" Power up. "You don't have to win for me to know how much you rock!" Pressure off. "God can help you do it, and I'm here too." Support.

He won the class contest. While he refused to present, he opted to introduce. I was more than OK with that. "Maybe the next one, Mom. Yes, I think next year if I win, I'll do the final thingy."

In fourth grade he won the class contest and presented at the finals without batting an eyelash, still as shy as ever but plowing through with the confidence of a president making his final speech before election day. He did not win, but I believe DS won in breakthrough.

One of the greatest things about breakthroughs, even small ones, is that we can revisit them and remind our children of God-in-past-successes to strengthen them for the next one.

Encourage, encourage, encourage. *"For I know the plans I have for you," declares the Lord, "plans to prosper you and not to harm you, plans to give you hope and a future"* (Jer. 29:11).

What You Can Do: Do not limit what God can do in your child's life. Make God big. Bigger than her problems, her feelings, her friends, her dreams, her hair, her body shape, her strengths, her weaknesses, her sins, her past, her future, herself, and you—bigger than life itself. Together, find a Scripture to stand on, a promise to hold, that will see you both through the seemingly impossible. See? You've bonded!

Noticing = Talk

It's vital to notice the good, the positive, and the beautiful things about our kids. I had DS convinced as a little boy that I had eyes in the back of my head. Of course, like most mothers do, I used my intuitive instincts, or what I prefer to term my "discerning" ability to catch him in the act of grabbing another cookie, pretending to brush his teeth, or about to pull the cat's tail—normal trivial childhood temptations. Recently, DS reminded me that I hadn't noticed that he'd done something without my asking him to. It got me thinking about how we need to use these eyes in the back of our heads to notice the *right* that our children do—not only the bad. How would it have affected his training up if I had used those extra set of eyes to spot the good?

God keeps no records of our wrongs. I have a feeling He doesn't go searching for them, either. Our sins are plain enough. If we parents notice the positive, I have a feeling that sin will be become plain enough to our children, as clear as green snot on a white sleeve.

At times it is hard not to focus on a C-minus in math when I know my child is capable of B's or better. But I stand the best chance of seeing his math mark improve by noticing the things he did right, like the "satisfactory" for effort, or the B he got in science, rather than reaming him out for the almost below average math grade.

We also have to train our eyes to see when our child is hurting, if something is bothering him, if he needs to talk, or is asking for space to work something out. When DS gets in the car after school, I know what kind of day he's had.

"What's wrong?"

"How'd you know?"

"Eyes."

Ponder This: Do you notice the things that are important to your child? What does she dream about? If we do not know our children, we cannot strengthen their dreams and set them up for success.

Time = Talk

I am so grateful that DS's school is a 20-minute drive away. Our time together during the 40 minutes of every day in the car is one of God's time-redeeming gifts to us. At first I did not like the thought of that long drive, and almost moved closer to the school, but I am so glad I didn't. It has been a parenting gold mine.

> *The car is where I discover the most about my son's life and where we engage in meaningful and positive conversation and interaction.*

The car is where I discover the most about my son's life and where we engage in meaningful and positive conversation and interaction. It also boosts his level of concentration and ability to focus at school as we sort out fears, challenges, and successes. The car is a frequent environment for his questions about faith. The simplest things that we see enroute can be fodder for learning. We have real quality time together, and we have both reaped rewards from it.

DS of course now is big enough for the front seat, which is great because often I'll take his hand and hold it, or reach over and touch his cheek. I also give him charge of the controls as my copilot. Anything outside of my driving space is his domain—air conditioner, radio, CD player, defroster, vents, glove compartment, automatic windows, rear window wiper, side-view mirror. This fosters our working together to fight heat, cold, frost, rain, bad music, and disorganization! He feels he is helping, and I encourage him as a copilot. "Thank you for helping us arrive home safely," does much for his ego.

Although my son balks about it, I take at least one evening a week, usually two, for recess with DS. A family night. He really does like it and notices if we skip a week. Take the time, spend the time, and devote more time toward building a strong relationship with your child. I know it's hard, but if we wait for time, it won't appear, and as I mentioned before, God will redeem our time. What is a half day with your child, balanced against the rest of life?

Model Moment: The key is to listen so that you can ask more questions about their day, feelings, and opinions. The objective is to engage your child's mind and heart beyond yes or no answers without interrogating! Interrogate and he will shut down and shut you down. Getting all the answers is not the objective. The goal is to get your child to talk to you, because together you can solve anything.

Conversation Starters

- *What was the nicest thing you did for someone today? That someone did for you?*

- *What was the best/worst thing that happened today?*

- *How was recess? What games did you play?*

- *Teach me something that you learned today that I might not know.*

- *In the next 30 seconds, tell me everything you did today!*

- *What would make today perfect for you?*

- *Who did you sit with at lunch today?*

- *If you could go on vacation anywhere in the world, where would you go?*

- *If you could have any kind of house, what kind would you want?*

- *If you could be a famous athlete, writer, artist, actor, or musician, who would you be? Why?*

- *If you could be principal for a day, what would you do?*

- *If you could be invisible, where would you go and what would you do?*

- *What is the meanest thing someone can say to you?*

- *If you had to give every person on the planet one quality, what would it be? Why?*

- *If you could invent one thing, what would it be?*

- *If you could know one thing about the future, what would it be?*

- *What do you look for in a friend?*

- *Describe the most beautiful thing you have ever seen.*

- *Who do you want to see in Heaven?*

Service = Talk

Give your child lots to talk about. Many of us are tempted to put our kids into sports, but why not into nursing homes or food banks? Involve your child in service. Helping others helps break the downward cycle of low self-esteem as a child learns how to communicate with people of different ages and backgrounds. As he busies himself focusing on others, praying, blessing, and serving, unhealthy concern for himself will gradually diminish.

Several years ago I was asked to check in regularly on a family friend's elderly mother whom he had placed in a nursing home for round-the-clock care. She had Alzheimer's disease and was recovering from a cancer operation. I knew Lois, we had been friends, and I was blessed to help. DS was 8, and still going through tough times adjusting to our family breakup. I wasn't sure it would be a good idea to "expose" him to people in physical and emotional pain.

One day I couldn't find a babysitter, and brought him along on my nursing home visit. To my surprise, Lois, who up to that point had not responded to anyone, smiled when I introduced her to DS, and began a conversation with him. The next time, DS asked if he could come along, "Please mom, I want to help GG." We met up with her in the dining room where she sat, just staring at her food.

"GG," asked DS, "why aren't you eating? You have to eat to get strong." He pulled up a chair beside her wheelchair, scooped up a spoonful of mashed potato, and held it to her closed lips. "Come on, eat," he urged. "For me." She smiled and opened wide. He spooned it in and continued to feed her until he was sure she'd had enough. It was the first real food she'd eaten since she arrived, and the nurses were pleased, praising DS for taking such good care of Lois. Over the next few weeks, he'd help her out of the wheelchair and into bed, wheel her to group activities, and run back to her room for a sweater if she seemed cold.

I can't begin to tell you what this did for him—and for Lois. He enriched her last days, and her family was grateful for that. Normally reserved, he grew bold in the nursing home environment, even assisting and chatting with other residents. He felt useful, capable, mature, and empowered to help others.

This did much for his feelings of acceptance, worth, and value. For the first time in a long while, he began to share his deeper feelings concerning the disruption in his life.

At school, DS would usually get picked last for things—always shuffled down to the least for team projects or sports. He suffered greatly for this, sensing criticism and rejection by his peers. He went through a period of feeling as if he could do nothing right or good enough. If he tried to communicate with classmates, they'd shun him, and when he clammed up, they teased him. "They just don't know you," I said. "If they did, they would know what a gift you are."

Joseph of the Old Testament knew exactly who he was, His relationship to God, and his worth in God's eyes. This knowledge helped him to act accordingly and to get through the severest storms (see Gen. 37-40). If your child knows his worth to God, his parents, and to others, he may view his peers as greatly mistaken. As his knowledge grows of his true self worth, so does evidence gather that his peers simply do not know him, and the truth emerges that he is not a bad person or a loser.

DS's self-esteem is constantly tested. When it is low, he makes poor choices and is unable to withstand the swift currents of peer pressure. Will your child be strong enough to resist blending in so that she does not stand out? Does she have the confidence to be who she is? At some point, our children will begin making their own decisions about who their friends will be and which values they live out. If we parents cannot communicate those values, their friends or the media will.

One teenager said, "Parents need to fill a child's bucket of self-esteem so high that the rest of the world can't poke enough holes in it to drain it dry."

Your assignment? Intentionally and fiercely love your child, build life, encouragement, and truth into her life, be involved, esteem her as a person whom God says is marvelous and a wonder, so that she has the courage to flex her mouth and faith muscles, and communicate and live an excellent life for Christ.

Family Devotions = Talk

As a single parent, I know how hard it can be to do any kind of routine formal spiritual teaching, but I also know that it is vital to daily teach my child about God.

Laurie, single parent of five children, shares that her kids get bored, complain, and resist devotional time. "For the most part, we have drifted away from it, and although it concerns me, I am a little relieved. I don't have the battle, and I have a little extra time for other things. But I do miss our time of openness...."

The Bible is where your child learns about God and how He desires her to live. It is where she hears life-changing messages *directly from God*. Does she understand the Bible as God's Word, His voice? No other book is like the Bible and no other book has impacted the world as it has and will continue to do so. Your devotional time should reflect that. Inspire and awe your child at what God did in the Bible and what He can do in her life!

Bring it home. Set the mood with music. Use visuals. Teach the Bible in a way that scoops her into the story. For that to happen, it must sweep you up, too. The goal is to inspire and to allow the Word's penetrating message to do the work. Then, when God's message settles into her heart, you help her use and apply that message to make a difference in her sphere of influence. Trust that when we impart God's Word into our children's hearts, His Word will not return void.

What You Can Do: I found it helpful to break out of the traditional method of devotional time at least once a week. Get creative. Find teachable moments that helps you bring biblical and applicable teachings about God into your settings. Don't allow even one teachable moment pass by. Weave God and His ways into as many aspects of your daily life as possible. Place several Bibles throughout your home. Refer to it often, as you would a television guide. Make Scripture come alive and make it applicable.

Visit a lake and talk about the parting of the Red Sea. Grab a slice of bread, cut it up into little pieces, and toss it up into the air. Watch it fall like manna. Have them follow you as you lead them through and around the house into special places, closets, the attic, as though they were the children of Israel on their way to the Promised Land. Go to a mountain and imagine Moses coming down from Mount Sinai with the Ten Commandments.

Discipline = Talk?

The right kind of discipline can improve communication between you and your child and build character and godly resolve. The "KFC" formula, that of being kind, firm, and consistent in discipline has gone a long way toward keeping my communication open with DS and toward helping me feel fuller as a godly, successful, and sane single parent!

Showing him *kindness*, *firmness*, and *consistency*, DS will tell me what I need to know when the cat suddenly freaks out.

It is difficult to convey boundaries or consequences if DS isn't listening. Conversely, if I cannot hear what he has to say, I will not understand why he has disobeyed, nor will I know how to react, respond, or incorporate an adequate consequence in a fair manner. As a result, he is apt to be tried by a hung jury, and I'll never know what really happened to poor Felix.

"Because I told you so," is not communication. Our children desire and deserve explanations at every age. If you don't take time to explain why an action was wrong, which is communicating, how will you ever get the child to the point of listening when you attempt to teach her what is right? When DS participates in a decision, he is much more motivated to carry it out.

"Because I told you so," is not communication.

First, always be *kind* and respectful toward your little tail-puller. The Bible commands fathers especially not to exasperate the child, even if the child exasperates the fur-ball (see Eph. 6:4). So how can a dad or mom exasperate a son or daughter? Crazed yelling will do it. Playing dictator will do it. Pulling off your child's leg will do it. Slapping the child around will do it.

Whippings will do it. A sharp cuff on the head will do it. Calling your child a "stupid good-for-nothing" will do it. Freaking out will do it. Curling up into a ball will do it. The silent treatment will do it. Threats will do it. Ignoring the problem will do it. Saying nothing will do it. Doing nothing will do it. Our children need admonition, yes, but not abuse.

I don't need to tell you about what respect is, since we've already covered that. But many of us, because of stress, weariness, and loads of responsibilities, sometimes disrespect our children by allowing ourselves to become doormats, or we become too dictatorial to maintain order and control. We react and overreact, and then regret our words, our actions, or our lack of actions regarding misbehaviors. We are the Rhett Butlers, frankly not giving a damn, or the Scarlett O'Hara's, moving the "I'll deal with it" forward to another day.

As a result, don't be surprised if Tara burns down. That is, communication fails. If this does happen, you will also see a tearing away of the heart of your relationship.

I show kindness to DS by dealing with what is going on immediately, in a sound, compassionate, and fruitful manner. Yelling doesn't cut it. He sees my lips move, but eventually all he hears is blah, blah, blah, and his eyes glaze over.

Conversely, kids who fight back or grow defiant will purposely sin just to get you back or hurt you. Oy. Kindness keeps my own behaviors in check and shows my love toward DS as unconditional. How I express my corrective guidance makes all the difference in how he receives it, and how motivated he is to correct it. I ensure that DS knows that although I desire and expect better of him the next time, that I love him no matter what!

Second, you should be *firm,* as in possessing resolute determination and strength of character, being steady, stable, and on firm footing, with sound judgment of a situation. It comes about by way of discernment, which is a gift from God and operates in grace and faith, through the eye of your heart where the Holy Spirit lives. It enables you to flow in agreement with God's authority and wise counsel, and to make decisions based on God's truth and not on your own opinions. In short, it is about agreeing with the heart of God on a matter. Suspicion and condemnation, which are rooted in falsehood, opinion, mistrust, rejection, or fear, fly out the door with the cat when I use discernment.

Godly Discernment

Godly discernment is not intuition, a sixth sense, a feeling, an educated guess, or weighing something based on the odds. Oh, it is much higher than that! Discernment hits its mark every time as you seek God's counsel, which is trustworthy, and you can fully depend upon it for every personal and parenting situation. It will enable you to understand the significance of why things are happening to your child—to see beyond the sin to the heart of the matter. It helps you know your child and what makes him tick. It helps you distinguish what is good and what is evil.

You will recognize a God-way and God's work when you see it. You will understand deeper spiritual truths and realities. You will be able to avoid the enemy's plans and schemes and therefore help your child be respectful. You will be able to effectively and firmly direct, inspire, counsel, and discipline. You will spot a ruse a mile away! Immediately, you will know that Felix did not pull his own tail, because discernment makes you wise—discernment and wisdom work hand in hand. What did Solomon ask of God? Wisdom. What did God give Sol? A wise and discerning heart (see 1 Kings 3:12).

We cannot discern without the Holy Spirit who is our Teacher and Counselor and who leads us into all truth, enabling us to understand. We also learn discernment through God's Word in the daily renewing of our minds in prayer. We operate in discernment through relationship with Christ Jesus. What a precious gift of the heart discernment is to us.

So, yes, as a parent, you can be firm. You can confidently spy out the land as you make prayerful reconnaissance trips into your child's heart, laying hold of a good overcoming strategy, and lovingly and wisely following through with it.

Which brings me to the third part of the KFC discipline formula: *consistency.* It won't happen without kindness and firmness, which is love and discernment. The goal in my discipline of DS is to help him choose an acceptable behavior and to learn self-control.

I often make the mistake of failing to follow through with a consequence, which invites a continuous breach of limits. If we don't follow through with a consequence for a pull-the-tail episode, by the end of the day that poor cat will be cowering under the sofa. And, we cannot discipline Johnny on Tuesday, and ignore a similar breach of limits on Thursday. Consistency drives home our expectations and saves the cat.

What About Spanking—Corporal Punishment?

Sigh. I knew it would come to this. So many discipline techniques and methods to choose from, and honestly, I don't have a doctorate in child discipline. I say, do what God tells you to do. But understand that God has never whipped *you* into submission! So be certain it is *His* voice you hear. Ask Him for His revelation and truth concerning your interpretation of His guidance in the area of physical discipline as it relates to your child and his or her unique needs, personality, age, predisposition, emotional, physical, and spiritual health.

> *Love must be the primary factor in dealing with any form of discipline.*

No, I'm not copping out by not answering the question directly! The thing to remember is that love is the greatest influence in the child's life and the driving force toward obedience. I would suggest the following. If you do not communicate well with your child, do not spank. If you do not exercise discernment, do not spank. If your child has low self-esteem, do not spank. If you do not have compassion, do not spank. If you do not understand your child, do not spank. If you do not know God and His ways, do not spank. If you do not love your child, do not spank. Love must be the primary factor in dealing with any form of discipline or the return is zip.

Natural and Logical Consequences

The use of natural and logical consequences do go a long way to improving DS's behavior. But first I had to understand how to correctly use them, and only if we were openly communicating! Note, in dangerous situations, please use your best discernment.

Some of us seek to punish when we should really let the natural happen. Sometimes, *natural* consequences happen without interference from me though I do monitor things. For instance, DS waited for me to fall asleep so that he could play his PSP under the covers all night; the natural consequence was extreme fatigue the following day. It was awhile before he associated these things, but he learned eventually that in order not to be tired, he needed his sleep. He became more apt to learn from his error in judgment through natural consequence.

Of course, I don't want to wait for a natural consequence if a behavior is disruptive, or if it harms or endangers DS. Suddenly falling grades because he cannot stay awake in class may mean he simply doesn't care about the consequence. Also, if the natural consequence takes too long to happen, he sometimes forgets what he did wrong and therefore, does not associate it. In this case, switching to a logical consequence is the rational way to go.

Logical consequences are what we impose on a child for behaving in a certain way. For example, if DS refuses to shut down the computer when I ask, his computer privileges are taken away. Grounding him from seeing his friends would not be a logical move. He needs to connect what he did wrong with what he has lost as a result. Often I am tempted to send DS to bed early for any infraction, but I see it for what it is, the temptation to have some free, quiet time for myself!

Disciplining Through Different Parenting Styles

It is common for children to negatively act out during a divorce and post divorce. I saw this in children in my daycare. They are greatly impacted by the anxieties and insecurities caused by the strife in their parents' relationship and by the upheavals in their lives. As bad as we may feel for our children, though, it would be a disservice not to follow KFC.

In DS's case, I continued to set rules and follow through, and I kept our communication and my observation of his emotions active, just in case he was feeling insecure or crying out for help and attention to his feelings. At one point, DS grew hot-tempered and verbally aggressive, but I recognized his behavior as what it was—acting out due to the big changes in our lives. If I had left it unchecked and not dealt with the underlying issues, he and I both would still be at odds with one another.

Communication and compromise between my ex and me have helped when making and enforcing rules and consequences for breaking them, although we do not agree on some points. This is not always easy, with one parent usually playing the role of "good time parent," and the other "the meanie," the one who attempts to regain control. This lack of consistency, often brought on by my guilt, confused DS. It helps if both parents come together, if possible, to agree on rules that apply in both homes, and the carrying through of a consequence as the child moves between homes.

For instance, DS did something that caused a punishment of no computer time for three days. However, he was scheduled to be at his father's home during that time. I called his dad and asked if he would please enforce it that weekend. He agreed and followed through. You and your ex might agree on consequences such as timeouts; loss of television, video gaming, or computer privileges; earlier curfew; or a moratorium on after-school play.

After a misbehavior and repentance, or even before repentance, I encourage DS to pray, because in so doing, he will know as he speaks to the Father through Jesus that he is still loved, cherished, and accepted. Prayer also gives us both time to reflect on actions, taking responsibility and accountability for them, because yes, sometimes his reactions are a result of something I've done or forgotten or overreacted about, and so I resolve to behave better.

If you are leading your child in prayer after disciplining him, be sure that he hears about his strengths and gifts and the positive choices he made during the process. Your prayer could go something like this:

> *Father in Heaven, Johnny has come to admit he pulled the cat's tail. I am so thankful that he had the courage to own up to it. Please help us both to work on hearing each other better and trusting each other more, remembering how important honesty and trust, kindness, and gentleness is in this family. Lord, I forgive Johnny. Thank You that Felix will be OK. In Jesus' name we pray. Amen!*

The "I Hear You" Formula

One day my own son busted me big time. "Mom, you hardly ever look at me when I ask or tell you something…." It was true. I had not been giving him my full attention, which conveyed to him that anything he had to tell me, say, or ask was not important to me. I was floored with sadness. *How long had I done that?* I asked DS to forgive me, and then I asked God's forgiveness.

How much harm had my turning away done? How often did I trade his gaze for an "Uh huh," "Yup," or "Just a sec"?

How often did I avoid his precious eyes, which are beautiful by the way—large, expressive, and they seem to change color with his moods. When he was a baby, I could not stop gazing into them.

Did he see more of my back than he did of my face? From that moment on, I determined to acknowledge him with respect. I would stop what I was doing, drop to his height, look at him face to face, and for at least one minute *listen*. Miracles of miracles, this new routine cured the badger and the whine. Now that he's taller than me, I have to stand on my toes, or I flop on his bed or sit beside him on the sofa. Always, I turn my head, stop what I'm doing, meet his eyes, and show genuine interest in my gentle giant.

Power Up: Don't trade the gaze for anything! How often is your child speaking to your back? You can put out many fires by learning to Stop, Drop, Look, and Listen.

PART III

Nurturing for the Lazarus Factor—*Raising Whole Kids*

CHAPTER 6

"Raising" Your Kids From the Dead

When I was young I was sure of everything; in a few years, having been mistaken a thousand times, I was not half so sure of most things as I was before; at present, I am hardly sure of anything but what God has revealed to me.—John Wesley

D o you have a child who is four days dead? She's still upset about the loss of a parent; she might be grieving, angry, rebellious, or apathetic. Has she stopped communicating? Christ will raise her as He did His friend Lazarus![30] God can perfect us! He didn't just raise Himself from the dead, He raised *us* from the dead too. This must be understood in the heart. If you, Mom or Dad, know that God raised you from the dead, you won't want to do anything but to become like Him, and you will know that you can become like Him. God promises that you and your children can become like Him.

If your daughter knows that God raised her from the dead, she won't want to do anything other than become Christlike, and she will know that she can. She knows that she can resist the temptations of promiscuity, because she has already experienced the power of God in her life. The resurrection not only applies to us now, but it is also an ongoing transformation. It changes us today. It comforts us today. It burns away our sinful passions today. The Kingdom of God is within you, the resurrection and life lives within you now.

Do What Matters Most

My ongoing goal is to get DS to understand with the eye of his heart how to live for Christ and walk the walk, not by his might or my might, not by his power or mine to help him over his grief, mourning, fear, trauma, or change—only by the power of the Spirit of Almighty God can he be whole.[31] The apostle Paul wanted to experience, even feel God's mighty power—so do our kids, because they feel totally powerless over their lives. We train, but the power from on high sprinkles the clean water on our children, pours on the miracle oil, gives them a fresh start, new heart and spirit, and removes their heart of stone for a heart of flesh, moving them to follow His decrees and be careful to keep His laws.[32]

Hope Future for *Now* Impact

What if you could teach your child to pull "hope future" (which, by the way, is supernaturally spectacular) into her *now* for powerful affect? It would help her process the trauma of divorce. It would help her process right from wrong. What would happen if you led and encouraged her in the spirit of Romans 8:9-11 power?

> *You, however, are controlled not by the sinful nature but by the Spirit, if the Spirit of God lives in you. And*

if anyone does not have the Spirit of Christ, he does not belong to Christ. But if Christ is in you, your body is dead because of sin, yet your spirit is alive because of righteousness. And if the Spirit of him who raised Jesus from the dead is living in you, he who raised Christ from the dead will also give life to your mortal bodies through his Spirit, who lives in you (Romans 8:9-11).

She would not be controlled by the sinful nature, but by the Spirit of God in her. She would be dead to sin but her spirit alive because of righteousness. The same Spirit who raised Jesus from the dead would give life to her mortal body.

Indeed, if you fill your own heart to believe God's loving transformational and creative power in *her* life, your words, reactions, and actions would reflect that hope seeped in the Father's love. As a result, rebellion and low self-esteem may gradually—or immediately—disappear. She may just pull "hope future" into the present for all that she has to deal with—rejection, peer pressure—and come to know Jesus and overcome. Kids want power and independence—why not introduce them to God's way early in their lives? His way is better than the world's way by a long shot.

Heart Check: Do your words and actions reflect transformational hope? Do you believe God can transform your child, protect and save her? Are you tilling the soil of your child's heart? The heart is the root of disobedience. Don't break her heart! Nothing can dash hope more than believing evil of a child, making false accusations, deflating her trust in your unconditional love and acceptance of her, constant criticism, not listening,

> threatening her with rejection, or even somehow communicating to her that she is unwanted, too much to bear, or that you will send her away. Threatening your child with rejection is wrong. Instead, communicate your approval. Build relationship with her. Take time to listen, talk, respect her feelings, and know her as a person.

The Very Best Is Near

Unless our children believe in another life after this one—and not half life, reincarnation, New Age gobbledygook—it will be difficult for them to see why they should be kind, honest, or loving in difficult or challenging circumstances. If the resurrection miracle does not live in them, they will not have transformation to look forward to. They will expect to fail, be cheated, be harmed, and die, so what's the point? I'll do my thing; it won't make a difference. They will live to satisfy themselves and they will be manipulated by those who want to turn and twist their minds and wills.

On the other hand, if they have and live their being in Christ Jesus, they will expect that whatever struggles they are going through today are just passing things, challenges they can get through with Jesus for a greater glory.

Gaby's Story

Little Gaby Davis, a girl in my son's class in elementary school, went on to glory in 2007 after having suffered terribly with an aggressive cancer. I got to know her briefly one day when I filled in for her daycare giver who was tending to an emergency. Gaby was the sweetest, most angelic little girl I ever met. She had a honey-love presence about her, a light that seemed to follow her around the playroom, and later, around the school.

Her illness and death shocked and devastated the children and teachers at the school, the family's many friends and relatives, and, of course, her parents and three brothers, who adored her. I'm sure many wondered why God would permit this wee one to suffer so, but those wondering people didn't have knowledge of the greater glory coming to her. I wondered myself, "How can the parents endure watching their beloved young daughter's body waste away, and then the devastating void left when she went to be with the Lord?"

I attended her funeral, and then I knew. Gaby, little Gaby, even at 7 years of age, believed in the resurrection power of Christ Jesus and the transformation of her body. She believed in the end of pain and suffering and the beginning of an eternal life. She believed that her entire being was in Jesus, and that she would be with Him for eternity. Everything to do with her future was ultimately about Jesus—she wanted everyone to know she was going to an amazing place, and she hoped she would see her loved ones there soon.

In the photograph that accompanied the obituary, clearly taken during her illness, Gaby was described as a "spunky little princess...now with Jesus and her beloved cat. She wore a bandana tucked behind her ears, and appeared pale and thin, but her smile was wide, revealing two beautiful, shiny front teeth, and her eyes, well, they were bright with promise."

Cure for Morale Decay

Hope is necessary in this unsettling world because it brings inner peace. Our children have so many questions and inner conflicts that there is no way we alone can settle their hearts or satisfy their deepest whys. Some children have been rejected by a parent. They do not know what it is to be loved by a father.

They need to know what it feels like to have God awaken their hearts with a healing kiss, their faces pulled close to His, hearing Him say, "Wake up and live!" They need to experience this, know what it feels like to be parented and led by the Perfect Parent, experience the emotion wrought by fatherly love, feel it, even display it. Their hearts need to be wildly beating for God, secure in Him, experiencing the embrace and wonder of His love and power moment by moment, anticipating forever with Him—this is the greatest security they have.[33] You, Mom or Dad, come in a close second!

The promise of resurrection future and present as seen through the heart of the Father's gift to humanity, His only Son, Jesus Christ, His death, and His resurrection, gives children undying and unwavering hope.

Many children in single-parent families—yes, even solo *Christian* families, OK, dual parent nests too—are lacking hope and as a result, are suffering moral decay. Moral decay is the by-product of decomposition of the morale, and *morale* decay must be addressed first. DS fought many battles—the worst ones, internalized and spiritual, he did not have the words to describe. Often, bad behavior, anger, rebellion, addiction, or depression were the result.

My son, oh my goodness, fell into depression when he was only 10 years of age! He internalized everything; not intentionally, but he just didn't have the words to describe his heartache and frustrations in a way that anyone but God could understand. Until he could cry it all out to God, his heart just kept imploding.

Suicide is prevalent among our youth. Why? The eyes of our children's hearts have no understanding of the hope of salvation and the hope of life to come. For the most part, adults haven't modeled hope, lived hope, or lived expecting miracles and transformation, especially in the more mundane aspects of this present life.

Your child can face uncertain days because Jesus lives!

I was guilty of this. My own worries overcame me, and as a result, I made God out to be very small to DS. I wasn't living:

Because He lives, I can face tomorrow, because He lives, all fear is gone; because I know He holds the future, and life is worth the living just because He lives.

Bill and Gloria Gaither wrote those lyrics during a difficult time. The miracle of their son's birth inspired and poured gratitude out of their hearts.

How sweet to hold a newborn baby, and feel the pride and joy he gives; but greater still the calm assurance: This child can face uncertain days because He lives.

Question: How big is your God? If God is not in your present life, what would His absence make your child think that God could be in her forever tomorrow? Likewise, if God's power is not evident in your home today, what would make your child believe in God's power at all, except for God's sovereignty? If we trust God for the small, we will build up our own faith for the greater needs, and our kids will more likely follow suit. If we cannot believe God to cure a cold, how can we believe God to cure a cancer? If we cannot believe God for the ten dollars we're short, how can we believe Him for next month's rent? If we cannot ourselves believe in a God who has an interest in the smaller, less consequential things concerning us today, how can our kids believe that God has any interest in them whatsoever?

Single parents, our kids are hurting. They are asking, "Does God really care about me?" If we cannot count on God to transform a bad circumstance, how can they?

With no such hope or example, the mind-set might be: "It won't make a difference if I sleep with Sally. Why should I be kind, honest, love the poor? Why not bully Jimmy, lie, steal? Why not take drugs, jump off the cliff...the only thing ahead of me is a dead end anyhow. What has God ever done for us—for Mom, Dad, or me?" In other words, if there is no hope, why stand for a principle under threat—there would be no profit and no point. Blessedly, it's not like that. You *can* face uncertain days because Jesus lives!

Youth Problems: Cover Ups for Deeper Hurts?

Youth binge drinking is a real problem today—many die as a result of alcohol poisoning. What are these young people drowning out? The voice of the enemy tells them there is no hope, no heavenly reason why they should not drink, lie, steal, have premarital sex, cut themselves, swear, lash back, rebel, quit school, hurt a brother, or rob a store.

Tattoos and Body Mods: What's the Message?

Young people are getting tattoos—beyond cute little butterflies, hearts, and flowers in inconspicuous places. Why? Some are walking ink pads covered with everything from tribal bands to barbed wire strands. Are those who are excessively tattooed getting inked because they do not love what they see in the mirror, and are trying to cover it up? Is their self-esteem that low? The findings of a psychological study suggest that tattoos are not just a fashion accessory. Tattoos in excess may be driven by a wide range of motivational factors, significantly tied in with a person's self-esteem. Reasons why people get tattoos include rebellion and wanting to belong to a group. People having three or more tattoos are likely to have low self-esteem.[34]

Are these children trying to send parents or God a message about what really hurts inside? Are youth crying out to know who they are? Cracked hearts, skulls and crossbones, dragons—sometimes just one image on the skin can tell the story of what is going on inside a heart. Curt, age 16, a respondent in an online tattoo forum, writes, "I like the way tattoos make me feel, never better! Every time I get a new one, it is like finding a missing piece of myself...."

The choice of a tattoo can clue a parent in to how a youth is feeling about life. The image may memorialize a life high or low. One anonymous youth writes that he got his first "tat" at age 17, a Tasmanian devil as the grim reaper, on his right back shoulder. Online correspondent Rebecca plans to get a tat of a spider cartwheeling into a night goddess—this from a spiritual dream she deems significant enough to hold "desperately and deeply close to my heart."

Other "body mods" are going on, such as piercings and plastic surgeries—perhaps from low self-esteem? A research paper cites that tattoos reflect hopes, values, or beliefs, and act as vehicles to communicate those beliefs to others. For some people, tattoos offer a means to reclaim a sense of ownership and control over their body, or to explore their identity through experimentation with their outward appearances.[35]

Examine the Evidence: If your child is into tattoos, even washable ones—it may give you a clue to what's going on inside.

Gaming/Internet Addictions

Some of our children get lost in addiction to computer games, and parents as well. One game, World of Warcraft, is an interactive immersive world that one recovering youth describes as "so much better than real life." It wreaks havoc on many adults, young people, and increasingly computer savvy younger children. One young gamer recalls, "My warrior was a monster and a beast feared by the horde and respected by the alliance. An awesome dwarf full of rage, skill and energy; so unlike I was in real life; I could barely move...."

Do you know that there is a whole Website dedicated to being a World of Warcraft (WoW) detox center, where over 40,000 people have confessed to the detrimental affects of this game's addictiveness in their lives? Check it out at www.wowdetox.com.

I'll let you in on a secret. Internet gaming addiction was a big factor in the breakdown of my marriage and our family. It is serious stuff!

Alert: Do you know anything about what your child is playing on the computer and why? With whom they are playing? What strategy is involved? Are there occult factors, a violence rating, restrictions, a language rating, and/or ungodly factors?

If It Goes *Poof,* Then What?

Today many children are starved for supernatural spiritual power with which to navigate their lives, but many are staring hell in the face. We are losing many of them to fantasy and occult games, among other things, which give them a false sense of empowerment and control of their destiny, a false and ultimately empty sense of identity, and an unrealistic escape from responsibilities and burdens—and scary, scary answers to problems.

For the first year or so of my singleness, I allowed DS, who was on summer break, more time on the computer than I should have. He got caught up in an online game, and spent hours in virtual reality while I scrambled to meet an important book deadline that would pay the following month's bills. At the same time, I was purposely trying to forget the pain of the past and the fear I had of the future, through immersing myself in work.

Every day, he'd tell me about his accomplishments: the powers he earned through play, the stuff he had amassed, and the control that he had. He had dictatorship of a world and the highest scores. I thought, "OK, he's happy; it can't be all that bad for him." One afternoon, I heard a bloodcurdling scream, "NO-o-o-o!" I ran into his room, thinking he'd fallen back on his chair and hit his head or something.

"What happened?" He'd thrown himself on his bed and was pounding the pillow, sobbing wildly.

"Someone got my password and stole everything—my identity, my stuff, my score…it's all gone…all for nothing Mom!"

It took him days to rise from his personal crash. The game had empowered him at a time when he felt his real world was chaos and falling apart beyond his control. And this virtual world, one he had created for himself, had fallen apart. Honestly, I myself was despairing and void of hope for a season, so he truly did feel powerless, bless his precious heart.

Watch for signs that your child is trying to gain a feeling of control over his life or fill an emotional void. He definitely needs God, personal attention, additional prayer and intercession, a positive role model, and/or, if symptoms are severe, immediate professional medical and spiritual help. The following are only a few of many symptoms or signs that your child needs help:

- *Too much computer, television, or gaming.*

- *Acting out frustration in a physical manner.*

- *Holding in frustration.*

- *Lethargy, apathy, despair.*

- *Not wanting to interact or socialize in real life.*

- *Outright rebellion, defiance.*

- *Crying, weeping.*

- *Unable to or doesn't want to sleep or eat.*

- *Unable to or won't concentrate on a task.*

- *Rejecting you, fighting with siblings.*

- *Distaste for the Word of God.*

- *Neglect of personal hygiene.*

- *Overtly flirtatious, physical.*

- *Stealing, associating with unsavory friends.*

- *Fearfulness, nightmares.*

- *Afraid of his or of your death.*

- *More than a normal interest in Heaven.*

- *Tattoos, piercings, cutting, body mods.*

- *Drinking, using drugs.*

Can They See God at Home?

Could the problem be that we are not showing God to our children in our homes? If they don't see Him at home with them, is He absent from their reality?

Listen, our kids are struggling with *"wild beasts in Ephesus."*[36] They'll even fight Goliath or a million Goliaths if they have something personal worth fighting for, which can only be the result of Christ in them, the hope of glory.

Too many kids are way down, far beyond their power, past their strengths, and down so deep they are despairing even of life. They can't get up. What's wrong? The apostle Paul who had at one time made it his life mission to kill those alive in

Christ said, "I despair of life." In effect, he was saying that he faced a death sentence. But God came on the scene and delivered him. Having experienced an incredible miracle, Paul said, "I have been resurrected from the dead." The Lord took him out of the grave, he stared hell in the face, and God resurrected him.[37] God will "raise" your child!

How's Your Resolve? If you are despairing of your single situation, guaranteed, so is your child. If you feel you are facing a death sentence, guaranteed, your child feels that way too. However, guess what happens when you believe in God to raise your dead resolve? Right! He resurrects your hope, and raises your child's hope in the process. You know what to do!

Doing What Matters for Eternity

Many of today's teenagers and even children have become hopeless, with no clue why they are alive, where their lives count, and whether there is a purpose for being alive. Scan the faces at school and you can't help but notice dejection. Listen, it's easy enough for me to fall into hopelessness just seeing world conditions worsen daily or watching the spread of diseases.

When our children feel the squeeze as they become adolescents, they tune out things like teachers, parents, authority, and empty religion. They may turn to escape routes including Internet gaming, drugs, sex, or parties, among other things. These pursuits can lead to an overwhelming number of social and parenting problems. Houston, we (and they) have a problem—especially if they are telling you:

- *You don't own me!*

- *Your (blip) rules are stupid!*

- *I don't have to do what you say!*
- *I don't choose your friends, so you can't choose mine!*
- *You don't want me to have a life!*
- *Who cares? You don't!*
- *I'll do what I want, and there's nothing you can do about it!*
- *Get a life, Dad. I'm not your little girl anymore.*
- *You're the one who needs God, not me!*
- *Lay a hand on me and I will turn you in for child abuse.*
- *Stay out of my room!*
- *Curfews suck.*
- *I hate you. I hate God. I hate my teachers…*
- *Life sucks.*

Most articles and books concerning today's youth are written from an adult perspective. What do young people themselves say are their greatest concerns today? Ask your own child, "What's on your mind?"

My son's concerns? There were times he thought we were not listening to him. He was afraid to speak to his dad about things that troubled him because he feared teasing or negativity. He shared recently that he did not want to be a burden on me. He was afraid of what would happen to him if I died. He is afraid that nobody likes him. These express the types of worries on the minds of today's children.

> *As we communicate with God concerning our children, He will teach us the way into their hearts.*

We definitely do not want our world-weary children tuning us out or tuning out the Lord. We simply cannot risk a communication block between ourselves and God, for one, or between ourselves and our children, because we are their lifeline to God. As we communicate with God concerning our children, He will teach us the way into their hearts. If their doors are closed, finding entry can be a daunting task. Our job is to keep the doors open as we lead and teach our children how to connect themselves with God and with us. Their lives depend upon it.

What You Can Do Now: Become a sower of hope. Rise above what you feel and model, and live out hope, knowing that depression may easily and quickly take hold of your family. Your child is chosen, loved, forgiven, alive, complete, and victorious! Feed truth because the truth will set him free!

Never Too Young to Come to God

We must lead our children—yes, even the youngest ones—to the greatest Force early. They are never too young. They must learn now what it means to be caught up in the life of Jesus, for then they will experience the life-giving resurrection flow of His grace to be shaped by the journey of faith. It is He who passes onto them a power mighty enough to tear down the forces of hell and produce abundance where there is lack.

Many parents unintentionally forsake their children by assuming their little ones are not mature enough to know the truths that God has revealed in His Word, and of their need for a Savior. Don't forsake them in this, because God loves them from birth and even before. If Christ died for all, which the Word says He did,[38] no one is exempt, not even infants. And since salvation is appropriated by faith in those old enough to do so, there must be some other way in which the saving power of Christ's death is transferred to those too young to have personal faith.[39]

Consider the evidence of the Lord relating intimately to babies:

- *"...from my mother's womb you have been my God."*[40]

- *"From birth I have relied on you; you brought me forth from my mother's womb."*[41]

- *"Listen to me, O house of Jacob...you whom I have upheld since you were conceived, and have carried since your birth."*[42]

He even made provision for babies, those not old enough to believe or commit themselves to God.[43] By way of the New Testament, we know how the Holy Spirit can come upon a child in the womb or from birth, and of their having a special relationship with God. Consider "leaping Johnny." Of course, I am speaking about John the Baptist who leapt in his mother Elizabeth's womb when she heard Mary's greeting, *"...the baby in my womb leaped for joy."*[44] It was prophesied that *"...he will be filled with the Holy Spirit even from birth."*[45]

Elizabeth was filled with the Holy Spirit, and when Mary, carrying Jesus, neared the other expectant mother, her baby John recognized Him, and leaped for joy.

If we are filled with the same power, our children, no matter how young, will recognize the presence of Jesus in our lives and homes, and respond with joy accordingly. Moreover, they will thrive in the presence of the Lord amidst enemy onslaughts, and live with Him in relationship.

Flea Alert: The enemy wants your children. This is not reason to be afraid, because greater is He who is in them than he who is in the world.[46] Satan is aware that your children will shape the coming generation and have great potential to become powerful history-makers with God. He may be more subtle than he was in DS's case, and you may not even realize his plan, but at least make yourself aware of his tactics even if everything seems OK right now.

Dedicate Your Children

The act of dedicating children to God was a common practice of blessing among His people in both the Old and New Testament times. Additionally, it was a statement of recognition of the parents that their child truly belonged to God. As Christians today, we dedicate children with the same purpose in mind. Dedication is a public expression of faith and commitment on our part, and of blessing on God's part through His Church.

This act by us is a prayerful declaration of our stewardship over God's gracious gift of our children to us. It is also our pledge to do what we can as God gives us wisdom to raise our children to respect and honor God the Father in Heaven and to love and serve His Son, Jesus Christ. A dedication celebration is more than a ritual—it is a covenant or a commitment on our part to honor the will and the Word of God, to affirm our personal faith in Christ, and to renew our own dedication to Him and His Word. This is arranged through your pastor.

What You Can Do:

- *Recognize that your child belongs to God and has been born to experience God's love and to serve Him with all of his or her heart.*

- *Pray daily for God's direction in your life and in your child's life.*

- *Faithfully participate in church activities with your child.*

- *Teach your child the truths of God's Word in your home.*

- *Gently and swiftly lead your child to personal faith in Christ.*

- *Seek to know God. Stay in the Word. Pray and believe.*

Children do not like to be in the dark; they need that night light on all the time. If you are flowing in the power of the Holy Spirit and His presence is in your home, this can be enough to keep the devil out of it. In a way, your home is like the womb and like being in Christ's heart; your kids are hidden there. Even in the womb and as infants, our children can sense the presence of evil and equally the power and presence of God.

God will not forsake the helpless. Your faith and prayers activate His power to a greater degree to render the enemy ineffective and speed healing in the areas where your infant, child, or teen has been hurt. As you stay in the Word and learn more about the Lord, your discernment concerning satan and his works and plans will increase as will your ability to apply God's power for immediate, profound, and lasting results. In a God-infused atmosphere, your child or children will know that they can do all things.

Leading Your Flock to Jesus

When he could talk, I led DS to Jesus. He asked God into his heart by repeating the sinner's prayer after me. Not long ago, he rededicated his life to God, prayed on his own to receive Jesus into his heart, and recorded and sealed his commitment in pen in the front of his Bible. To celebrate, we stayed up all night to see the sun rise, and afterward went to the donut shop for breakfast. Later that day (after a good sleep, mind you), we commemorated the event by starting an avocado plant with a pit suspended in a jar of water. We had heard that they grow to be beautiful plants that could even be transplanted outdoors. It will take a few weeks to root, and we water it every day with expectation of what it is to become.

In the same way, I look forward to that day when DS will become as a mighty oak, firmly planted in the Lord, fruitful, and withstanding inclement weather and the logging plans of the enemy!

How can you be sure if your child is established in Christ? Evaluate what flows from your older child or teen's heart in tough circumstances, such as losing a best friend, having a fight with a sibling, handling a canceled visit from the other parent, having a privilege taken away, when a loved one gets sick, and so on. Does he trust Jesus to make it better, to open another door? Does she fight fair believing in God's justice? Does he hold grudges? Does jealousy flare? Rage? Backbiting? Bitterness? What about the three I-words my Granny used to use—is he impertinent, impudent, insolent?

Power Up: When your child hides herself with the Risen Christ in God, she leaves the merely human sinful sphere and enters into the divine sphere of "anything is possible," and "I am more than a conqueror." When trouble, temptation, weakness, sickness, worry, or anxiety arises, she will find the risen Lord leading her to glory.

A Parent's Greater Joy

The joy in my heart the night my son rededicated his life to God even surpassed the joy I experienced when he first lay in my arms as an infant. As great as that early time was, this spiritual rebirth was a greater joy, knowing that my child would be with me in eternity. This added so much to my future hope! In addition, I knew for sure that his would be a life of overcoming power for what is ahead in his teen years and for the time he sets out and is on his own. He now has the help of the Holy Spirit, the One whom Jesus said He would send to those who believed in Him.

More importantly—the *top* reason why you should feel compelled to pray for your child's salvation is so Jesus will be glorified by his or her salvation granted in answer to your prayers. Prayer for your child's salvation motivated by that foremost desire is power prayer!

Hearing your child ask Jesus into his or her heart is more than music to your ears—it is an eternal leaping in your womb and peace of heart. Moreover, when you stand before God, you can proclaim with confidence and boldness that you have made your child aware of her own sinful nature, have shown her the need for salvation, and taught her about the Redeemer. You can say, "She has repented from her sins, called upon You, confessed Jesus as her Savior, and committed her life to serving You. I have been faithful to teach her Your wonderful and holy way, Lord."

There is no greater delight, dear parent, and it is my prayer that if your child is unsaved, that he soon come to know that saving power, not only for him, but for you, too—nothing refreshes like the blessed assurance of Jesus! The most important thing you can do is to influence your family's choice to have a second birth in Christ. You and your child will still have challenges—but you will have a tangible way through them: the *assurance* of God in the midst of your problems, the *confidence* of God ahead of you in battle, and the *joy of knowing* that He really does have your family in His hand.

It doesn't mean our job is finished, not by a long shot. Every day we must grow in relationship with God. We must prepare as a family for an eternal passionate relationship with the One who is the Way, the Truth, and the Life—learning how to trustingly jump into His arms moment by moment.

You are Vital to Their Rebirth

The best person to lead your child to Jesus is you, the parent! Why? First, it might not get done if you leave it to someone else. Second, God does not place this training obligation on anyone other than the child's parents (or guardian). We are commanded to bring our children up in the reverent fear and nurture of the Lord.

Of all of your priorities right now, pray for your son or daughter's salvation. Your child will live eternally, but where? When children are very young, before the age of accountability, God is merciful and they go to Heaven. But the time comes when your older child faces God.

Nobody Knows Them as You Do

Have others intercede for your child, but don't depend upon them alone. Few people will prioritize your child as you do. No one else can plead for her as you can. Why? Because no one on this earth loves her as much as you do! Who, other than you or the other parent perhaps, has the tenderness that you have for your child? Who, other than you, knows your daughter's make-up as you do, areas of weakness, strength, sensitivity, or insecurity? No one but you. It is up to you.

Moreover, in Heaven, who but God the Father knows your child's needs and loves her even more? He hears your plea and responds. The prayer of a parent to *the* Parent is powerful. If you know how to give good gifts to your child, how much more will your heavenly Father give the Holy Spirit to those who ask Him (see Luke 11:13).

We have His great and precious promise:

> *But the mercy of the Lord is from everlasting to everlasting on those who fear Him, and His righteousness to children's children, to such as keep His covenant, and to those who remember His commandments to do to them* (Psalms 103:17-18 NKJV).

It Is Not Too Late! Salvation is a great prize and worth every hour you spend on your knees believing for it and securing it. Pray as you instruct. Pray as you model. Pray as you discipline. Pray with perseverance! Pray as she sleeps. Pray as she wakes. Pray in between. Let her hear you pray! Prioritize prayer for her salvation, and she will come to God young, before she develops wrong habits and while she can still develop godly ones. Give her the determination to fight and repel sin as the world increasingly rises to welcome her. The earlier she knows Jesus, the easier your work, because the Holy Spirit will empower her to respect and obey. But if your child is already in the pimple or first whiskers stage, fear not—with the God of second, third, fourth, or even fifth chances, it is never too late to lead your child to Him.[47]

In Touch With God

My Salvation Prayer for Your Family:

Heavenly Father, I come before you on behalf of my reader's family. You know his or her heart for the very best. You know all things and see all things. Moreover, You see their potential for overcoming and victorious greatness in You. I pray Lord that every member of his or her family will see the light of Your Son, that Your tangible presence will shine so brightly as to cause a hunger, thirst, and curiosity such that they cannot deny. As You enlighten this parent with revelation and inspiration from Your Word, I pray for that heavenly burning desire within her or his heart to know more about Jesus, the Savior of the world. I declare in Jesus' name that the enemy has no hold on my reader's family, and I ask that every accusation made against her or him will be washed away by the blood of

Jesus. I bind the demonic influence that would hold this parent back from receiving Your Son as Savior. I declare Your Word over this family that today, salvation has come to this house. Gather them up in Your glorious presence, and let them experience the deepest love that only You can give. May they receive this precious gift You so freely give that they may love and serve You all the days of their lives, glorifying You, causing the world to wonder how apart from God could they have overcome so much. In Jesus' name, Amen!

Straight Up: Knowing the Lord and loving Jesus Christ His Son with all of your heart, mind, and soul should be the *foundation* for what you do and the choices you make for your child. You are not preparing him to succeed in life as much as you are preparing and leading him for eternity—giving him the hope in Christ he so desperately needs. What shall it profit your child to gain the whole world but lose his own soul (see Mark 8:36). His very life depends upon eternal relationship with the Lord. Don't worry about offending your child! You will beat yourself up really badly one day if you haven't at least shown him the way.

What You Can Do Now: When we pray, we surrender power to the Lord over all situations and over the child we lift up to God. Yes, God is already in control, but praying shows Him that we understand our need for Him, and that we are aware of His authority, power, and grace. When you pray for your son or daughter, boldly claim God's goodness in all things, no matter the outcome. When you pray, pray faithfully, truly releasing your will and your child's will to God's ultimate will. When you pray, pray sincerely, showing your love for your child and for your Father in Heaven. Urge salvation with gentleness, compassion, and delight, modeling, encouraging, comforting your children to live lives worthy of God, who calls them into His Kingdom and glory (see 1 Thess. 2:6-8,11). They have everything to gain if they do, and everything to lose, including their lives, if they do not.

Wedge Your Way In

Our window of influence shrinks every day, more so in this modern age when children grow up quicker than ever as the world sinks its teeth into them. Donna, a neighbor with three children, is afraid that because she works outside of the home and is so busy afterward, that she is missing opportunities to provide what her children desperately need in terms of teaching them about the Lord, including validation, affirmation, love, and guidance—just for starters!

"Sure I get dinner on the table, and help them with homework, but I sense that if I don't somehow learn how to effectively and consistently provide for their emotional and spiritual needs, that it will only be a matter of time before they seek these truths elsewhere…from wrong people and bad influences."

Indeed, how can she impact their lives if she is not around as much as she needs or wants to be?

We must be diligent in wedging ourselves into our children's lives and intentionally and actively parenting them rather than resorting to default conditioning—with too much reliance on our feelings, experiences, upbringing, easier paths, and even our present realities—if we are to experience true success in our Christian discipling efforts. This takes maximizing the time that we have, using teachable moments to our advantage, and taking every opportunity to wedge our way in at all cost.

Lead Your Little One to Salvation

Dear God, thank You for dying on the Cross to take away my sin. Thank You for making me a child of God. I know that I am a sinner because I have done some wrong stuff, and I need You in my life. I trust Your promise and I want to live my life for You. Please forgive me. I believe that Jesus died for me and rose from the dead, and I ask Him to come into my life to be My Savior and Lord. Show me how to live, and give me Your precious Spirit so I will do what You want me to do. Help me when I do the things that You do not want me to do. Keep me trusting You every day. Thank You so much for loving me as You do. In Jesus' name, Amen.

The Holy Spirit

The moment your child accepts Jesus Christ as her personal Lord and Savior, the Holy Spirit comes to dwell within her, joining with her spirit (see 1 Cor. 6:19). The Holy Spirit will help her discern right from wrong. He will give her a strong desire for the truth and guide her into all truth, showing her things to come (see John 16:13). He brings comfort, enlightenment, illumination, and understanding of God's Word, as well as a hunger for righteousness.

The Baptism of the Holy Spirit

A child is never too young to receive this precious gift from the Lord, whereby the Lord may also give him a special prayer language all his own (see Mark 16:17), which helps to further strengthen his relationship with the Lord, building him up in faith. The baptism of the Holy Spirit and with fire (see Luke 3:16) is a wonderful gift Christians receive after salvation. It is not a requisite to salvation but a separate gift.

The baptism of the Holy Spirit should be a natural part of your child's experience. It is a gift from God the Father in Heaven who is the ultimate Giver (see Luke 11:13). Being baptized in the Holy Spirit is God's way of helping us to experience more power, more boldness, and to understand in a greater and more profound way His presence in our everyday lives. It immerses us in the Holy Spirit's life and power and gives us the desire for more of God in us. "Blessed are those who hunger and thirst for righteousness, for they will be filled" (Matt. 5:6). The baptism of the Holy Spirit is a great empowerment that reproduces the ministry of Jesus (we shall do great and greater works) to heal the sick and cleanse the leper, for signs, wonders, and miracles. Whenever DS prays for my "owies," I get healed. No fooling!

Jesus commanded us in Acts 1:4-5 to be baptized in the Holy Spirit. The Holy Spirit gives us power to be bold witnesses for Jesus, strengthens us, helps us to be what God wants us to be, and do what God wants us to do (see John 16:13), and also helps us to pray as God desires us to pray (see Rom. 8:26-27).

Set Your Child Up to Want It

This beautiful experience of a special prayer language is a gift, but your child must be willing to submit fully to God to receive it. Jesus will respond to a totally yielded vessel and will never ask more of your child than she is capable of giving, nor will He ever fail to give her something greater in return, when she does give her all!

Ask your child if she would like Jesus to baptize her in the Holy Spirit, if she would like a new spiritual prayer language all her own to help her communicate with God the deepest things of her heart. Don't pressure. Just ask. If she agrees, go ahead and lead her to ask:

Heavenly Father, I thank You that Jesus saved me, and I pray that the Holy Spirit would come upon me. Jesus, please baptize me in the Holy Spirit so that I can have the power to be a bold witness for You. I receive the baptism in the Holy Spirit by faith in Your Word. May the anointing, the glory, and the power of God come upon me and into my life this moment, and empower me for service today.

Now, having asked and received, have your child practice the power of the Holy Spirit in the same manner in which the apostles did, by praising God out loud in whatever words come to mind. Have her tell God how much she loves Him, thanks Him, and worships Him.

Fill my mouth and my heart with praise to You. Thank you for giving me the ability to speak in a language I have not been taught. Help me to use it to glorify You and to grow me into who You desire me to be, for Your glory.

It may just happen that she opens her mouth and makes strange sounds, laughs, or cries. Encourage her to utter whatever she hears in her mind. She may do it quietly or loudly. Encourage her to use her prayer language every day, wherever she is, silently or in her private times, while she walks, in the car, before she drifts off to sleep.

Water Baptism

Water baptism (the dunk-a-roo, not the sprinkle) is a public profession of faith when she can share God's goodness in her life with God's family as she is submerged in water just as Jesus was baptized by John the Baptist. For sure, your church family and extended family members will want to celebrate your child's commitment!

Growing in Faith Basics

Encourage time alone with Jesus through reading an age-appropriate Bible, and through song, worship, and prayer. Encourage your child to attend church and/or Sunday school faithfully with you. As she grows in faith and in her walk with the Lord, she will have opportunity to share her commitment to Jesus with others as well. Help your child understand that a lifelong walk with Jesus will have some ups and downs but she can be assured that He will never leave her and will always be ready to forgive and to move on. Jesus truly is the Way, the Truth, and the Life.

Teach Your Child to Pray

Teach your child how to give thanks and praise and find comfort by developing a personal relationship with God through ongoing heart-to-heart conversation (prayer). This is a gift that will carry your child through life. Prayer is more than, "Now I lay me down to sleep...." It is more than a rote prayer in a prescribed setting. It is a service of the heart that encourages an awareness of the world around us.

Here are some thoughts about prayer and ways I've encouraged my child to pray:

- *I let him catch me praying. This shows him that I love God, that I am human in admitting my wrongs, that I am working through sorrow and expressing joy at God's goodness in my life. My prayers have demonstrated to DS how to be reflective of the things that touch his life, too. In short, I am creating and cultivating a prayer culture in the home, praying through everything, and not limiting prayer only to bed or mealtimes.*

- *When I drive or as we watch the news, we "flash-pray" as things happen, for people in ambulances or those waiting at bus stops.*

- *Never skip mealtime grace because a guest is present, you are in a restaurant, or on the fly through a drive-through. There is never a reason not to thank God for bounty!*

- *Help your child understand that the purpose of prayer is to talk to God. Encourage honesty and openness with God. Prayer should include the good, the bad, and the ugly—everything can be taken to God. It is powerful to tell your child there is nothing that she cannot say to God, no feeling she can't share in prayer. A fumbled heartfelt prayer is more meaningful than an eloquent one. Drop the thee, thy, thou, whither goest, and pretenses. Let her know that God already knows her heart. If all she can do is say one word, God knows the rest. She will graduate from one word to a string of words soon enough. Encourage your child that she is not praying to satisfy anyone, but as a means of communicating and building relationship with her Father in Heaven.*

- *Encourage prayer through song, dance, artistic expression, journaling, and praying in the spirit.*

- *The Lord's Prayer is a prayer example—not a rote prayer recital!*

- *Have your child lay hands on you or other family members for healing prayer, no matter how minor the ouch or how major the illness.*

- *Encourage a time of listening for God's response.*

- *Pray the Scriptures together.*

Teachable Moments: Show your child God within your present situation. You have shelter, you have food, you are safe, you are making friends—credit it all to God. Share with your child times when you have prayed and received answers from the Father in both small and dramatic ways. Tell true stories about others. Tell stories about people in the Bible who had their prayers answered.

Model Moments: Pray for those who hurt you. To pray for the salvation of someone who has deeply hurt you is one of the greatest images of Christlikeness that you can model for your children. Someone once told me that I would know if I have forgiven my son's father if I could imagine him saved and living forever in Heaven, perhaps even in proximity to me. This was a wake-up call to pray for his salvation, because only when I could do that could I truly release forgiveness toward him. To pray for those who have hurt us may be difficult, but the rewards are eternal. If we can model it, our children will be equipped to know how to deal with bitterness toward bullies and yes, even with the perceived wrongs of his or her parents.

CHAPTER 7

Freeing David—*Raising the Value Quotient*

When my children open up to me about an imperfection, or a fear, or a deep concern of their heart, they are letting me see them for who they are. I want to embrace them, and not SHAME them, so that they know they are safe with me.—Audrey Meisner[48]

When I hug my son, I don't let go until he does! Sometimes he lets go quickly and other times he holds on for dear life. I have the nail marks to prove it. The longer he holds on, it seems, the greater his emotional need at the moment. Bless his heart, he goes through such mixed ranges of emotions every day as his self-esteem takes hits from negative influences. Sometimes trying to motivate him is like squeezing water from a rock.

I concur with Audrey Meisner; I want to embrace my child so that he knows he is safe with me as he is. Some days, however, no matter how often I encourage DS or love on him, it seems it is not enough to convince him of his worth and value, that in my eyes and in God's eyes, he most certainly, definitely, assuredly measures up and then some!

Be Aware but Not Afraid of the *Hug Thug*

The devil is an identity thief who wants to rob our children of knowing who they are in Christ by luring them into a worldview identity. You see, he knows that if our children grab hold of who they are and who they will be in Christ, they not only will have a solid foundation upon which to build and live their lives, but they will also be very aware of the spiritual blessings of their inheritance immediately available for an overcoming life that glorifies God.

> The family is a microcosm of what God intended the Church to look like. In our families we should allow our children to think and experiment. They are still attached to us, but as we nurture them, we must allow them to grow and to come up with new ideas, thoughts, and plans. Jesus is knocking on the door of each heart. He has something that is unique for each person to accomplish in the Kingdom.[49]

Freeing David

There is a story circulating that I have not been able to confirm as true or not that goes like this. In the 1500s, the great artist Michelangelo chipped and chiseled his way through a block of rock that we know today as the sculpture of David. When he had finished, someone asked him how he could create such a masterpiece from the slab. He claimed that the masterpiece was already in that rock; he simply removed the excess stone so that David could escape. He called it *imagine del cour,* "heart's image." He said that he envisioned the heart's image, seeing in his mind's eye the finished product of David.

This is how God sees our children, and how we should see them *imagine del cour,* as the finished glorious product. In a sense, we are working backward in the same way God does. *"For we are God's workmanship, created in Christ Jesus to do good works, which God prepared in advance for us to do"* (Eph. 2:10). Parenting, therefore, can be viewed as chipping and chiseling away the excess stone so that our kids can escape! See who God has prepared them in advance to be, and help them break forth into it. Brilliant! Using this idea, whenever DS has feelings of doubt concerning his worth or his value, I remind him too of that finished product, constantly affirming what God showed me concerning him, that he will one day have the wisdom of Solomon, the heart of David for God, and the love of the Lord for humanity.

Grab Your Chisel!

Many of our children lack healthy self-esteem. They do not see themselves as masterpieces beautifully created by God. As a result, they fall into temptation and the world is swallowing them up. Most single-parented children have been through great emotional upheaval, with the loss of a parent through divorce, death, desertion, or separation. Hearts have been broken, leaving fertile soil for rejection to root.

Any crisis or circumstantial upheaval in a child's life can erode self-esteem: rejection by a parent or sibling, the death of a loved one, the loss of a best friend, a move, a new school, a failing grade. Even something as seemingly harmless as being turned down for a date or getting a pimple can be a crisis to a young person. Feelings of low self-worth can be the result of one or a combination of factors and sources.

Toddlers are more apt to act out their frustrations, but as children get older (at least I found this true of DS), they tend to internalize things, so signs might not always be as evident as say, throwing a tantrum is.

Chip Away the Demoralizing Voices

Kind words can be short and easy to speak, but their echoes are truly endless. —Mother Teresa[50]

Daily demoralizing voices surround and assail DS, and they are hard for him to ignore or shake off. The enemy with his lies, peers, the media, Hollywood, video games and computer games, and, even the church and his dad and I, can cloud, blur, or lower his self-worth quotient. With negative words, comparisons, ideals, societal norms, perfect pictures, family status, and religiosity, our kids may feel like they don't measure up, aren't liked, aren't good, talented, attractive, worth spending time with, or that they aren't accepted and heard. I'm constantly trying to help DS deflect confusing influences in his life because often they distort his view of how God sees him—as beautiful, His most precious creation, highly prized treasure, with amazingly infinite, eternal potential.

What You Can Do Now: Speak encouragingly and carefully to your child so as not to exasperate him (see Eph. 6:4) or cause him to become discouraged. What you say to your child may stay in his heart for a lifetime. If it is harsh and demeaning, his wounds may never heal. Too often, single-parented children become the verbal targets of our anger, frustration, and stress. They deserve our respect always.

What You Can Do: I challenge you to read the first three chapters of the Book of Ephesians in the New Testament where Paul describes at least 20 blessings—and read and teach them often to your child for a healthy dose of God's esteem. He will see his worth from God's view, be assured of His love and care, and will know that every good gift from God—every talent, every strength comes from Him. As deeply as I love DS, and would lay down my life for him, I know that God cares about him so much more.

Check Yourself: Low self-esteem was something I grappled with in my marriage toward its end. I felt rejected and not good enough, attractive enough, capable enough, talented enough… hello…I was a walking pillar of fear, lighting (or should I say darkening) the way for DS even though I constantly affirmed him in the Lord. Praise God, I take the proverbial bull by the horns now, and I am confident in whom God made me to be, so that I can do the impossible for my son, through Christ. I have a depth of understanding into the heart of God for me; and this deep-unto-deep conviction I can pass on to DS for even more glorious outcomes.

Do I feel guilty? Oh, sometimes I have to give the devil a swift kick, because I know once forgiven there is no condemnation for those in Christ Jesus. Sure I am sorry that I did not know better, and that my son has suffered as a result, but God does bring about good if we allow Him to, and our circumstances today can lead to a much better tomorrow. So, how are *you* feeling?

Power Up: As I mentioned in an earlier chapter, it is always good to have an open-door policy for God. He shouldn't have to knock all the time!

Modeling a God-View

When he was a toddler, DS easily soaked up the love and encouragement I gave him, even with two mind-sets parenting him (worldview and God-view), but when he hit kindergarten, his self-esteem took a downward turn after he discovered that he was not the only apple in the box.

"The teacher didn't pick me to erase the blackboard." "Matthew pushed me and called me a dweeb." "Everybody draws better than me." "I don't have any friends."

One of my research participants, single-mom Cindy, shared that when her son Sam was young and the family was still intact, there was tremendous imbalance in her home. Her husband dealt with their son negatively.

"If Sam misbehaved, John would say things like, 'What are you, stupid?' I tried so hard to build Sam up, to repair the damage, and usually I could because I spent the most time with him, but those negative words became so much louder to him as he grew up...he felt rejected by his father, and then the stealing started..."

Patterns of self-esteem and self-image appeared to start very early in DS's life as he developed thoughts about his own capabilities and self-concepts based on messages received from and interactions with adults and older children in my daycare and life situations. These either negative or positive patterns affected the choices and decisions he made while yet a "sponge."

I noticed with most of the young children in my daycare how readily they absorbed and responded to the messages they heard most often. One little girl who didn't socialize well eventually came out of her shell not by coaxing but by a positive reinforcement of how precious she was to us as part of our "family." She could finally see herself as I saw her, and developed feelings and behaviors consistent with that message of value. We are accountable for modeling and helping our children develop a healthy God-view of who they are, loving, encouraging, valuing, and nurturing the thought and belief that they are and always will be the apple of God's eye, and our own. Ultimately, that feeling of true acceptance without having to prove anything at all will keep them true to their values.

Evaluate: What messages does your child hear most often? What does your body language say?

Self-esteem Is a Choice

As DS matured out of toddlerhood, and even today, increasingly, accountability for a healthy godly self-esteem falls upon him. True self-esteem is ultimately how a person decides to feel about him or herself, apart from negative or contrary feedback. I am constantly telling DS that, at age 13, he makes the conscious choice to either accept or reject what people say about him, because he knows how God feels, and that should make all the difference.

This confidence is an inner work of godly confidence that results in obedience and ultimate adherence to values. I provide DS with the building blocks of love, care, encouragement, and environment conducive to a godly, healthy self-esteem, but he has to connect them into a foundation upon which he will live his life. It is not bought, found, or given, but the result of his choice of relationship with God, doing the right things, obedience, thinking the right thoughts, esteeming others, and refusing to give in to pressures or lies contrary to God's promises. Unless he learns how to build up his own self-esteem with a convicting sense of unconditional belonging, he will be in for disheartening and potentially crushing disappointment as he goes out into a world that does not value, esteem, or love him as I do and as God does. There won't always be cheering squads to applaud or affirm him, and society will try to squeeze him dry of the healthy values and attitudes I have taught and instilled.

> **Model Moment:** Model, communicate, and encourage your child to see and receive from God's point of view who she truly is so she can separate, glean, and process truth from the lies. Identify areas where your child's self-value quotient might be low or at risk. Redirect inaccurate beliefs about herself before they root and become reality to her.

What You Can Do

As a parent, please immediately stop:

- *Sighing, shrugging, rolling your eyes.*

- *Saying, "You'll be the death of me."*

- *Giving your child the silent treatment.*

- *Criticizing, blaming, threatening, judging, or hitting your children.*

- *Teasing, belittling, embracing, putting down, demoralizing.*

- *Asking, "Do you love me?"*

- *Yelling, lying, bribing.*

- *Worrying.*

- *Towering over, controlling, bossing, dictating.*

- *Freaking out over small stuff.*

- *Preaching, lording it over, postulating.*

- *Publicizing his faults.*

- *Revealing his secrets.*

- *Treating mistakes as failures.*

- *Complaining about your child's mother/father.*

- *Arguing.*

- *False praising (children read right through it).*

- *Revisiting his mistakes to instill guilt or shame.*

- *Adding to the pile of his worries with your problems such as money woes, injustice.*

- *Expecting perfection.*

- *Being hard on yourself.*

- *And most of all, STOP what you are doing and listen.*

Our Kids L-o-n-g to Belong

The pressure to fit in and conform today is a real issue for DS, especially since he longs to belong. This desire often leads to making wrong choices, to succumbing to peer pressure. My goal as a parent is to equip DS to decide that being accepted by others is not worth risking sin that affects self-respect. He must learn to lean on Jesus to help him resist the pressure, and not become so well-adjusted to his culture that he fits into it without even thinking.

> *When I approach a child, he inspires in me two sentiments; tenderness for what he is, and respect for what he may become.* —Louis Pasteur

Unless we parents esteem our children as God does, set them apart as God does,[51] treat them as uniquely and gloriously different as God does, and cultivate their incredible potential for the good, they will never have the self-confidence in Christ to live their dreams beyond their wildest expectations, nor will they have hope to rise above the "conform norm."

Your child is destined to be more than a "kid-gone-wrong" society stat! She has *infinite potential* to burst out of the ashes of brokenness and rise far above loneliness, rejection, dejection, depression, stigmatized traits, and disadvantage to become an incredible groundbreaker far above societal norms, cultivating and fostering values, making sound choices, resisting negative pressure, and doing the right thing.

Armor Against Challenges

A healthy self-esteem combines feelings of being loved with feelings of capability. If your child feels sure of herself as a person, she will be better able to stand up to life's pressures, challenges, and negative influences, especially entering the teen years. Low self-esteem paralyzes and is often a root cause for depression and rebelliousness, and for negative behavior such as drugs, stealing, lying, Internet addiction, sexual promiscuity, vandalism, alcohol, or running away. Self-esteem is the value we place on the mental or inward picture we have of ourselves. It is a collection of beliefs or feelings—our self-perceptions. How we define ourselves greatly influences our motivations, attitudes, and behaviors.

> *Children who feel good about themselves will have an easier time handling conflicts and resisting negative pressures.*

Check Your Child

Is your child friendly and kind to himself? Does he have confidence and faith? When DS feels good about himself, he often asks for help, for instance, or makes a concerted thoughtful effort in an area of struggle. If he is not feeling great, he tends to retreat from problems, easily gives up, or becomes frustrated, blames others, or appears depressed.

The earlier you identify areas of challenge, the sooner you can work together to develop a healthy pattern plan for a "can do" attitude. Sometimes the signs are direct, while other times the signs must be inferred from behavior and the ways in which your child copes. A good way to assess your child's self-worth and confidence is to observe how he or she responds to mistakes or failures.[52] The first in the following list, was one of the key clues I found in DS's behavior.

Possible Symptoms of Low Self-esteem

- *Denying a problem exists as a way of managing worry or pain.*

- *Doing poorly at school.*

- *Frequently failing in sports or other activities.*

- *Yelling, loud.*

- *Verbally or physically abusive.*

- *Avoiding new activities, people, or challenges.*

- *Hates trying new things.*

- *Berates self, calls self names such as "stupid, ugly, loser, dork, dweeb, gay."*

- *Quits as soon as a problem arises.*

- *Frustrates easily.*

- *Lies.*

- *Cheats to win.*

- *Steals.*

- *Curses, cusses.*

- *Spends much time in bedroom.*

- *Doesn't want to go to school.*

- *Hard to awaken, to get started into the day.*

- *Apathetic—simply doesn't care when others hurt, or about injustice.*

- *Overly reactive—often seeking vengeance.*

- *Overly helpful, compulsive perfectionism.*

- *Explores occult, religions, New Age thinking (searching for meaning).*

- *Is bossy or controlling.*

- *Bullying.*

- *Negativity, entertains little hope for success.*

- *Tattoos, piercings, cutting or hurting self.*

- *Goes "Goth," dyes hair, lots of black clothing.*

- *Wears sexually revealing clothing.*

- *Cakes on the makeup.*

- *Neglects personal hygiene.*

- *Suddenly starts a secret diary, is very protective of it.*

- *Suddenly won't communicate with parent or siblings.*

- *Everything becomes private, "my space."*

- *Makes remarks about God not being real, present, or caring. "If God had…"*

- *Accident prone.*

- *Addicted to fantasy games: computer, video. Watch out specifically for games like World of Warcraft, Dungeons and Dragons.*

- *Frequents social Internet chat sites, won't share details of online friends.*

- *Makes excuses and/or blames others for his own failure.*

- *Has difficulty receiving or acknowledging praise or compliments.*

- *Is overly concerned about what others think of her, doesn't want to look stupid.*

- *Says things like, "I always lose, always mess up, always fail, never do anything right."*

- *Doesn't think she is as important as others, her feelings don't matter.*

- *Takes it hard when passed up for something.*

- *Constantly feels he is wrong when someone challenges a belief or opinion.*

- *Thinks she has no friends—who would want to be friends with me?*

- *Clowning behavior to cover up his insecurities.*

- *Thinks she is too short, tall, fat, skinny, hates body features.*

- *Is easily influenced by negative pressure, runs with the crowd.*

- *Is uncomfortable in social settings, dislikes group activities.*

- *Does not work well independently.*

- *Is not optimistic.*

- *Fear or terror about making a mistake or failing at things he does try to do.*

- *Doesn't feel she can bail herself out when she has a problem.*

- *Doesn't smile or laugh a lot.*

- *Passive, withdrawn.*

- *Says, "I can't," when you know that he can.*

Alert: If your child is experiencing one or a combination of these possible symptoms of low self-esteem regularly or with increasing frequency, and efforts to change the behaviors or alleviate negative feelings are unsuccessful, immediately seek emotional and spiritual counseling from qualified mental/physical health and ministry professionals, since many of these symptoms can indicate depression, attention, or learning difficulties and are not to be taken lightly.

These symptoms may also indicate that your child is experimenting with or into drugs or alcohol or other abusive substances, has joined a gang or a wrong group of friends, or there are other causes of concern. This is not a complete list of warning signs. Without fail, learn more concerning depression, learning disabilities, and the signs of drug and alcohol use. Family, school, and child counselors can work to help uncover underlying issues that are preventing your child from feeling good about herself.

Some SUICIDE WARNING Signs

Even for professionals, suicide is difficult to predict, and all warning signs should be taken seriously. GET IMMEDIATE PROFESSIONAL HELP from your family physician, a mental health professional, a community mental health unit, or even the emergency room of your local hospital, if the child is at immediate risk. And, as that help comes, ask God to give you wisdom and strength concerning your child, for His protection over her, for healing, and for restoration of her hope. Foremost, assure your child of her loving and compassionate ever-present heavenly Father who is always ready to give her a reason for living. This list is not exhaustive! So be alert to any changes.

- *A desire to tell, referencing statements about suicide.*

- *A preoccupation with death, might even include questions like, "Will I go to Heaven if I kill myself?"*

- *Talking about hopelessness, worthlessness, saying things like, "You would be better off without me," or, "I wish I wasn't born," or, "If I wasn't around, your problems would disappear."*

- *Loss of interest in activities and people he or she once enjoyed.*

- *Giving belongings away.*

- *Calling people to say, "Good-bye."*

- *An increased use of alcohol or drugs.*

- *Inability to properly cope with a stressful event such as divorce, breakup, death of a loved one, loss of a friend, a move, a sin, a consequence of sin, guilt.*

- *Declining performance in school, at home.*

- *Extreme sadness, dejection, apathy, anxiety, or irritability.*

- *Social withdrawal and isolation.*

- *Neglect of personal care.*

- *Change in eating/sleeping habits.*

- *Reckless behavior, running in front of cars, taking risks.*

- *Previous suicide attempts.*

- *Sudden interest in weapons such as knives and firearms.*

- *An abrupt change from depressed to happy that may signify resignation to find relief in suicide.*[53]

Your child is chosen, loved, forgiven, alive, complete, and victorious! Feed truth—truth will set them free.

What Kids Think or Say—What You Can Say Back

I fail at everything: You have been chosen and appointed by Christ to bear His fruit, that whatever you ask of the Father in His name, He may give it to you! (See John 15:16.)

I don't feel like Jesus is living in my heart: You have been established, anointed, and sealed in Christ, and have been given the down payment of the Spirit of God in your heart! (See 2 Cor. 1:21-22.)

I hate myself: You have been given a holy calling. God saved you not according to what you do but according to His own purpose and grace, which was given to you in Christ Jesus before times eternal. (See 2 Tim. 1:9.)

If I do that, they will laugh at me: You have boldness and are not ashamed. (See 1 John 2:28.)

I can never forgive myself: You have passed from death to life in Christ. If you hear His word and believe, you have eternal life and don't come into judgment, you have passed out of death into life. (See John 5:24.)

Nobody likes me: You are free from any condemning charge against you, forever free from condemnation, for the law of the Spirit of Life in Christ Jesus made you free from the law of sin and death. If God is for you, who can be against you? God justifies you. Christ makes intercession for you. (See Rom. 8:1-2; 31-34.)

I don't deserve...: You have been forgiven in Christ, redeemed, and are a recipient of His rich grace. (See Eph. 4:32; 1:7-8.)

I could never be as good as...: You are complete in Christ. (See Col. 2:10.)

I'm trying, and I'm afraid of what will happen, but I just can't stop...: You have been given a spirit of power, love, and self-discipline, not fear! (See 2 Tim. 1:7.)

It's hard to believe anyone could love me: If you remain in His Word, you will know the truth and the truth will make you free. (See John 8:31-32.)

God just seems so distant: You are a son/daughter of God by the Spirit of adoption, and you can cry out, "Abba, Daddy Father!" (See Rom. 8:14-15.)

I hate how I look: You are a temple of God, His Spirit lives inside you! (See 1 Cor. 3:16.)

I have messed up too often: You are dead in your sin and alive with Christ and seated with Him in heavenly places, because by grace you are saved and have been raised up with Christ. (See Eph. 2:5-6.)

Prayer Changes Everything

How often and what do you pray for your child? As discussed previously, prayer is the best thing we can do and has the greatest effect. Pray for her character development, physical and emotional safety, relationship with God, for her other parent, step-parent, friends, for her future friends and spouse, her grades, opportunities, and personal struggles. It is never too late to pray.

God can heal past wounds, touch the present, and give her future hope. She benefits when you turn to God and place every detail of her life in His glorious hands. Prayer helps us to confidently see ahead of today's realities, and helps us be proactive for tomorrow. When your child sees you pray, you make a great and lasting impression on her. Praying is not just to change things; it is about God changing our children's hearts so they can influence the world.

Six Ways to Pray for Your Children Right Now

1. Pray that your child will develop a strong self-esteem rooted in the realization that she is God's workmanship. (See Eph. 2:10.)

2. Pray that she will always be strong and courageous in her character, values, and actions. (See Deut. 31:6.)

3. Pray that she will be content in every situation, confident in God who gives her strength. (See Phil. 4:12, 13.)

4. Pray that she will have an overflow of hope and hopefulness by the resurrection power of the Holy Spirit. (See Rom. 15:13.)

5. Pray that she will thirst for God, that she will desire streams of living water. (See Ps. 42:1.)

6. Pray that she will not faint, lose heart, or give up, but will be committed to prayer. (See Luke 18:1.)

Aim Heaven-High

Our children have been through a lot. We owe them the very best shot at developing themselves to their fullest and giving them the best opportunities to achieve God-soaked enthusiasm for a joy-filled life in this, at times, daunting single-family status in a postmodern society. It is time to present to them every advantage freely given by their heavenly Father. To hold back at all would be a grave injustice to them. Go for the maximum God has for your child. Don't let your child merely slide into first base. Give her what she needs for a home run. Help her faith become more than escaping hell and getting a ticket to

Heaven—give her the ride of her life. The world may call us disadvantaged, but we have God's Upper Hand.

Now that we've rooted out one of the biggest challenges facing single-parented children today—low self-esteem—let's get to work with passion and purpose, convincing our kids they are a gift and heritage of the Lord.[54] Let's encourage them to trust God, inspiring them to invite God to completely transform their minds and thoughts, to soar in their spirits, and conform them into His glorious image—rather than living a lifestyle that simply blends in, that bends under pressure, that compromises convictions, or that even gives up.

PART IV

Defying the Odds God's Way

CHAPTER 8

Never Give the Devil a Ride—
He Will Always Want to Drive

...God somehow, some way can turn [challenges] around for good. A lot of people say, 'Why are you still standing? How are you still standing? Why are you coming back for more?' You know what? God strengthens me through the challenges and allows me to stay very, very grounded because of my family and my kids, reminding me of what's important every day.... I always have that foundation of faith that I can stand strong on and hold on to, to get through challenges. My faith in Christ is really, at the end of the day, my be all end all.—Sarah Palin[55]

Even though life looks different from what you anticipated, even though single parenting was not your plan for an abundant life, single parented-ness does not have to keep you or your child from a rich, wonderful, joyful, peaceful, safe, protected, incredible life. God can work out all things for good. God will fulfill His promises for you and move you and your family into a rich new season of abundance in all things—moral values, spiritual fruit, love, faithfulness, respect, courage, health—yes, even if you are paying out a high percentage of your income in spousal support!

Children Have Destiny

Every child is a miracle, a heritage from the Lord. Remind yourself of that as you discover the tattoo your daughter has been hiding, when you feel you've "lost your child to the world."

Children have a special status in God's Kingdom; Jesus held them up as an example to adults. When asked who was the greatest in the Kingdom of Heaven, He answered the question by placing a little child in the disciples' midst. (Read Matt. 18:3-5; 19:14; Luke 9:48.)

Fight Me, Fight My Heavenly Gang

Because you and your child have accepted God's plan for your lives does not mean that satan backs off. He does not give up, because he knows that one Spirit-filled Christian walking in faith and miracles can deal a huge blow to his dark kingdom. He's dumb in that he has been defeated and his destiny sealed. He just doesn't believe it and doesn't want you to believe it, and will target your child, because your son or daughter has Kingdom of Heaven status, is greatly loved by God, and has the potential to do great exploits for God and His Kingdom even as a youngster! This is why it is vital that you and your child know how to bust satan's butt, call the shots, and rain big time on his evil lie of a parade. You have all of Heaven backing you up.

Power Up: When our children are young, it is up to us to deal with the enemy and keep a constant hedge of protection around them and around our homes. Even if our older children have not yet accepted Jesus, we have authority over satan's involvement in their lives, over everything that threatens their welfare and well-being, with the weapon of the Word, with the covering of the blood, and with the authority we have in His name. We also have the backup of angels as reinforcement. Trust God ahead of you and the army behind you to set the devil to flight.

Fear Not

Don't be afraid; just be aware. If you know the powerful authority you and your saved children have as blood-bought, born-again children of Almighty God, if you are not ignorant of the enemy's devices, if you know your enemy and his diabolical tactics and know the power of the blood of Jesus and of His Word, you can deal with the enemy as the flea he is. Jesus gave us authority to *"trample on serpents and scorpions and to overcome all the power of the enemy."* Further, He promised in the same breath that nothing shall by any means hurt us (see Luke 10:19). Nothing shall *by any means* hurt your children. Notice the action. Jesus gave us authority. This requires action on your part. Imagine Jesus handing you a scepter. Accept it. To *trample* is to crush, flatten, walk on, stamp on, tread, walk over, squash. Hey, I am no Johnny Appleseed. I squash anything that slithers or crawls (except babies) into my sphere.

Clean Your House

The best way to dispel darkness is to turn on a light! Here's how. When you bless your dwelling, you take authority over it because it belongs to you, and you are dedicating it to the Lord. Invite the Holy Spirit to come, and tell everything else to leave!

When you bless your home, you make room for God to take up residence in every room and over all possessions.

Spiritually, you determine who and what has access, *"…But as for me and my house, we will serve the Lord"* (Josh. 24:15). Your authority in Jesus' name determines the atmosphere. Just as the blood was applied to the door posts on Passover night, you may want to apply oil to all the doors and windows of your home. As you go from room to room, ask the Holy Spirit if there is anything in that room that grieves Him. Pray over each room, asking God to use it for His glory, thanking Him for providing you with a place to live. Ask for His angels to be posted at every entranceway and window. Out loud, say that you are countering any curse in the house with the blood of Jesus and you are taking authority in the name of Jesus. If you find a particular spot in the home that feels disturbing, stand on it and speak peace over it. Then invite the Holy Spirit to fill that space. "I speak peace here in the name of Jesus. I invite You to come, Holy Spirit, and fill this space. Fear (or whatever) leave in Jesus' name." I even anoint my son's computer with oil—as an additional and very powerful entryway into my home.[56]

I even anoint my son's computer with oil.

Don't be Distracted

A pastor friend, while praying deliverance over a mom for some generational stuff, discovered something profound as a particular demon started to manifest and speak through the woman. (Satan and his minions are *real*.) Speaking directly to the demon, the pastor demanded to know what holds were on the mother's son. The demon replied, "Are you kidding? She covers that boy in prayer—I can't get a hold edgewise!" Profound, eh?

We are especially vulnerable to enemy assault because most single parents are crazy busy, which is fertile ground for distraction from the things that build faith. If satan can get us away from prayer and God's Word, if he can render us neutral, apathetic, or fearful, he can get an edge. Don't give him the edge. However busy you are, take much time for God and adequate time in prayer over your family.

Prayer Covering Over Your Child

Oh, Father, You are the Great I Am and Immanuel, God with us in our midst. With You, nothing is impossible. I have seen Your mighty hand at work in our lives and I thank You for loving us as much as You do. In the most powerful and precious name of Jesus, the name above all names, I ask for Your Holy Spirit to come into this situation. I ask for divine healing in my child. I rebuke the enemy's attempts to steal from my child the childhood and life You destined him/her to have according to Your plans, Heavenly Father. I call forth your healing touch into my child. Please bring him/her comfort, peace, joy, and restoration, spiritual, emotional, mental, and physical healing. I know You are faithful, merciful, and loving. I pray for him/her and declare healing in Jesus' name. Thank You, God, for who You are and for the answers You are certain to give. In Jesus' name, Amen!

Truth! If you declare open season on the enemy—raise up a standard of prayer and protection, healing and deliverance, self-control and awareness—you will cut short the devil's heyday. There will be problems; the enemy will try, but God promises He will be in your midst and guarantees He will never leave or forsake His beloved ones (see Heb. 13:5). Even if your child seems irreversibly lost to drugs, homosexuality, anorexia, illness, promiscuity, low self-esteem, abusive behavior, is totally apathetic about the Lord, or is negative about anything purposeful, there is still *hope.*

As long as you are the parent and caring for your child, and you are abiding in Christ, your child is sanctified because you are sanctified. She is under your covering, your blessings. The blood of Jesus covers all. His blood restores all. That said, the reality of all that dark stuff, of the tactics of the devil and his cohorts should be our motivation to ensure that our own lives are completely surrendered to Christ's lordship. Unless we do, the devil has a portal into our family. And even then, he can enter in through other means.

When Slamming Doors Is Good

Before you can adequately loosen any footholds the enemy may have gained in the life of your child, *you,* dear one, have to close as many doors as you can to the enemy in your own life, tear down, and trample things attached to you that might latch onto your child as a result of a broken home, your brokenness, the sins of the parents, and even the sins of grandparents, great grandparents, and earlier ancestors. Why? Because one of satan's *primo tactos* is to gain access to children through parents. For instance, many of DS's fears seemed unfounded until I examined my own life and discovered many fears I had been unaware of. Once I determined the root of the fear and God expelled the darkness, my deliverance favorably impacted DS.

It is possible genetically for certain physical and emotional illnesses—cancer, depression, or schizophrenia, for example, to be passed on generationally. But do you know that many generational things are spiritual in nature? The sins of our relatives and even curses that came upon them can affect and perpetuate through multiple generations. There are some physical, emotional, and negative things, therefore, that happen to us that are not a direct result of something we have or have not done. Unless we oust them from our lives, they may cause our children more suffering than necessary.

If the enemy can get you, if he can stop God's purposes in your life, it may follow in the life of your child and leave you wondering why, particularly if you have loved her well, and she is still struggling. Your life may have taken a beating, you may be feeling fear and grief for the lost dreams and even ideals you once had. Your life can be so easily consumed by what is in the present that the past can make the disorder seem irreparable, and the future dry and barren. But God can restore you from your parched state, lift you up from the depths and restore you to even greater honor and comfort than you have ever known. He longs for your latter days to be greater than the former. His plan for you is your restoration so that you can effectively work with Him toward your family's restoration.

The following are twelve situations that may be plundering your abundance in the Lord, doors you will want to slam shut so that God can enter in and restore all that the evil one has taken away. Don't be surprised if your children are struggling with the same core issues. Dealing with yours will help you to identify and deal with theirs. Here's to mud *off* your eyes!

Identify Enemy Tactics

1. Lingering in *Past Hurts*

If you feel you have been treated unfairly or blame God or others for the things that don't seem right, you may not be able to trust God or others enough to move into an abundant life. It is easy to fall into a pattern of self-pity, lashing out at God. Satan uses discouragement to draw you inward, to keep you focused on your problems instead of leaning on God for support and strength. Ask the Father to help you come into a place of forgiveness. Repent and ask God to heal, soothe, and smooth over those rough places where you have been too wounded to move forward.

Trust God to love you enough to do regular foundation checks in your life to see where you really put your trust—upon whom you really are leaning, upon whose ability you really are relying on as you lay a foundation for your children.

God's Word got me through the really rough beginnings and sees me through each day. I never stopped believing that He had a plan for me, for DS, even for his father, because God is so much bigger than our circumstances. I knew one day that God could restore all that was lost to us, and eventually use my single parenting situation and my son's experiences to minister to others.

2. Lingering in *Fear*

Fears are like shackles that immobilize you, preventing you from taking your best foot forward, and from trusting God enough to reach beyond your present circumstances and into your future hope—the plans and purposes of God. A major mind-set I had to overcome was that of relying on my experiences and history to predict the future. This got me into a rut where I expected things would remain the same, or because I failed once in a relationship, that it would happen again. This fear wreaked havoc on my self-esteem and faith.

Learning from our mistakes and past has its merits and is common sense, but only to a point, in that we cannot let those things sequester our faith or dull our hope for the future. The fear of failing (again) may keep us from moving forward, and can be a real obstacle to focusing on the joy of the now and on tomorrow's joy, because we cling to what we know to be true of the past. I don't know about you, but there are some lessons in my life that were just so darned hard that I never ever want to revisit them, and fear prevents me from trying again. There are mistakes my parents made, and I do not want to take a risk that might lead me down a similar path for fear of repeating a mistake.

Lord knows we wrestle with enough problems today that we do not need to wrestle with the demons of the past (or present) that seek to rob us of our future! But we do tend to create tomorrow's problems by clinging to problems that do not or no longer exist. Let go! Conserve your energy; rally your faith for the genuine challenges ahead. Our mistakes are where God writes new scripts with incredibly happy endings:

> *"For I know the plans I have for you," declares the Lord, "plans to prosper you and not to harm you, plans to give you hope and a future. Then you will call upon me and come and pray to me, and I will listen to you. You will seek me and find me when you seek me with all your heart"* (Jeremiah 29:11-13).

I could write a book about the roots of fear, but many have already done it (see the Resources at the back of this book). For now, ask God to break the cycle of any fear immobilizing you. Learn how to assess your circumstances and situations, not from a lens of self-preservation, but through a Christ-centered view, understanding and embracing this great truth: no matter what you lose, no matter what you suffer, no matter the outlook, if you have Jesus and nothing else, you have more than enough and can genuinely say, *"I am so blessed"* (see Phil. 3:8).

3. Lingering in *Unbelief*

Unbelief holds you back from God's promises. It causes worry, fear, and anxiety. Unbelief says, "Oh sure, He provided for the multitude, but for me? I don't think so." Listen, don't allow the devil to kill your faith in God or to overlook the blessings in your life. Ask Him to restore your faith in Him, to identify and remove any areas of unbelief, or sin that holds you back from a full and abundant life. Of note—faith is not in trusting an outcome, but in unwavering trust and loyalty to God. It's OK to doubt, to ask questions, to probe deeper into the truths, but always trust in God's unwavering love, and remain loyal to Him, no matter what.

4. Lingering in *Unresolved/Unrepentant Sin*

Sin can rob you of blessings and can hinder God's plan for your life. Ongoing, willful sin has painful ramifications not only for you; it can also harm your family. Satan strives to convince us that what we do in private doesn't hurt anyone. This is a lie. Sin affects our attitude and behavior toward God and toward our family, and ruins our best laid plans.

> *Sin affects our attitude and behavior toward God and toward our family, and ruins our best laid plans.*

No way can any parent be effective in spiritual or any kind of sound leadership when sin abides unchecked. Worse, sin is the avenue through which the enemy gains entry to destroy lives. Please, don't deceive yourself by thinking that you can nurture and cultivate the spiritual well-being of your children while granting the enemy access into your home through ongoing sin.

The Bible says that we all have sinned and fallen short of the glory of God. However, as we apply the blood of Jesus to those sins, He cleanses us, and we can move on (see Rom. 3:23-26). If you are struggling with sin—addiction, excessive worry, bitterness, vengefulness—repent and ask God to reveal to you what caused satan's claw to give you vulnerability in that area. Ask the Lord to reveal satan's tactic, and for a strategy to remove his talons so that you can move ahead with gusto and expectation for God's very best.

Regain your sensitivity to sin so that you can sniff out where it has enslaved you. *First,* delve into Scripture. It will point out the sins that you hide deep down in your heart, and as you learn more about the perfect life of Jesus, will reveal where you have strayed. *Second,* build relationships with mature Christians who can objectively look at your life, and with compassion suggest where sin is at work (see also #11, Lingering in Rebellion). *Finally,* get away alone for some quiet and prayerful heart examination, and let the Holy Spirit lead you toward increasing holiness, widening the distance between you and sin. Be aware that sin will seek you out. If it finds you, take the Gospel Option. Getting back into God's Word and in touch with Him always increases my own sensitivity to sin. Understand that sin makes you sick, that Jesus is the cure, and that a life pursuing holiness will lead to increasing spiritual health and strength, rendering setbacks more rare.

5. Lingering in a *Lack of Knowledge*

If you don't know that God has a wonderful destiny planned for you, if you are unaware of the Holy Spirit and how He desires to move you forward into an incredible new season, if you do not know of the hope you have in the Lord, *get knowledge.* Get it through the Word, Christian folk, your pastor, prayer, listening to the Lord, and research. Whatever it takes, get the knowledge of God's great love for you. When you get such knowledge, yesterday melts away.

6. Lingering in a *Poverty Mind-set*

If you expect to live in spiritual, emotional, physical, and material poverty, guess what? Save for God's sovereignty in your life, don't be surprised if poverty hounds you. This was true in my own life—things got very tough, so that I almost resolved it would be my perpetual lot.

This mind-set kept me focused on my lack, blinding me to the promises of the Father for a rich future. Poverty says, "God cannot provide. I'll always be poor. I will never get ahead. I will never have enough. I will never experience abundance. Everyone is against me. The world owes me. If my ex hadn't done so and so, I would have such and such." The diligent are those who plan for riches and live with a heavenly, wealth-infused mind-set (see Prov. 21:5). They expect their miracles and do not mind waiting on God for them, waiting to see doors of opportunity swung open by God. They do not try to take matters into their own hands if something prayed for from God does not immediately appear.

7. Lingering in *a Survivor Mentality*

A survivor mentality can translate as pride, as trying to play God in your own life, of refusing to ask for help, of trying to do everything and control everything to glorify yourself. Pride says, "I'm a survivor," and it robs God of the credit and glory due Him. Excessive pride can also open the door to a poverty mind-set and fear, and definitely makes God appear small to the impressionable. Someone once said, "Nobody is more dangerous than a victim."[57] Pride can pump us up so much that we believe our accomplishments are our own doing.

8. Lingering in *Low Self-esteem*

Low self-esteem ties into a lack of knowledge and a poverty mind-set and is sin. Believing who God says you are in Christ is a choice, and if we choose not to believe it, we are deeming that God has told us an untruth.

9. Lingering in *Condemnation*

Many of us succumb to self-condemnation—a destructive tool of the enemy that causes guilt and shame where it is not warranted. If the devil can make you feel condemned or guilty over something small so that you linger there, it distracts from the bigger sin issues of your life or prevents you from feeling worthy enough to even approach the Lord about something.

10. Lingering in *Halfheartedness*

My ninth grade teacher, Mr. Guinty, called me "lackadai-sical" once and made me write the word and its definition on the blackboard a hundred times. I thanked him for the compliment, being the flower (daisy) child that I was! It is the best word to explain putting off doing something so that we can do something else. In other words, it is being *sluggish, passionless, lax, halfhearted, indifferent, spiritless*. I don't know many single parents who are lazy or lax in the sense of getting things done, but sometimes we put off doing what is right in order to accommodate our frame of mind, schedule, feelings of hopelessness, or even unbelief. We could be lax in getting godly knowledge because we don't want to know the truth, or halfhearted in not addressing an issue, say, of a child's computer addiction, because it acts as a babysitter and we have more time to ourselves if we put it off. We can easily fall into the trap of spiritual laziness, that of not praying when or what we should, of making no time for God's Word, or for fellowship with like-minded believers.

11. Lingering in *Rebellion*

Our teenagers aren't the only ones with rebellion issues. Many parents I know have this trait, especially with authority. However, we must ensure we have spiritual accountability to someone, somewhere on this earth, and submit also to those who are in authority over us in our daily lives, such as the government or civic authorities. For many Christians, our earthly spiritual authority is our pastor or a spiritual mother or father. Some of us still have our birth parents—but sometimes as they grow older we tend to reverse the parent/child roles. God has given us authoritative structures to save our hides more often than not, for protection, and for our well-being. We must learn to respect and submit to those structures God has placed in our lives. Foremost, of course, God should be enthroned in our lives, and we should be submitting to Him in all things.

12. Lingering in *Unforgiveness*

God, yourself, others. Need I say more about forgiveness? They spat on Him, lied about Him, beat Him, taunted Him, unjustly convicted Him, whipped Him, stripped Him, clubbed Him, disowned Him, murdered Him. Yet Jesus said, "Forgive them." Jesus had choices all right, and might (see Matt. 26:53), but He chose right so that goodness could spread.

Restorative Scriptures: Deuteronomy 30:15,19-20; Psalm 6:2-4; 71:20-21; 126:3-4; Proverbs 3:15-18; Isaiah 58:11; Jeremiah 30:17; Zechariah 9:11-12; John 10:10.

Understand: Forgiving someone does not turn you into a doormat. We should always call wrong "wrong," and seek courageous forms of resistance to it. It will surprise you to know that turning the other cheek is one form of resistance. However, the Bible doesn't say to turn it again, and again, and again. We should seek systems of justice to prevent pain and oppression when warranted, but also be forgiving—always forgiving. Forgiveness is a step toward true justice, healing, and restoration, for all parties involved. Refuse to take vengeance; that is God's job and His alone. Instead, believe that in the end there will be a resurrection, a judgment, and an eternity here on earth where weak is strong. In the end your sacrifices mean something. Praying for your foe means something. Love always wins.

Balance and Prioritize Your Time

Outside and personal interests and hobbies are necessary to help us stay sane, and to recharge and refresh; but we also have to carefully ensure we do not let things like the television or the Internet monopolize time that should be spent actively parenting our children. I always begin by asking myself if what I am doing is healthy, relevant, and balanced, considering the importance of devoting adequate time and attention to my son's spiritual, and for that matter, emotional and physical health.

The Bible tells us to be self-controlled and alert. It is hard to be alert to what is going on in my child's life while glued to the television or hooked for half a day on Wii Bowling. Ahem.

Recap: We are accountable for how we handle our role as spiritual leaders and protectors. If we are too busy for our children, if we are armchair parents, if all they see is our backside, how can we understand and remain alert to what is going on in their lives? Catch their eye.

An Invasion of Good

My Prayer for Your Family

Dear Father, let the enemy have not one in this family! Please invade his or her home! I pray for this believing parent and ask that You would give him or her strength to stand firm against the enemy. I ask that You send him or her a remembrance to daily clothe in Your full armor, and that You would give him or her words of wisdom and knowledge to share with the family. Let the light of Your Son Jesus shine brightly from him or her, so bright that his or her children's eyes must open. Please send Your angels to protect him or her from all demonic activity surrounding his or her environment. Send ministering angels, please, to whisper in his or her ears words from You that will bring him or her confidence and peace, knowing You are in control, present, longing for relationship, and that You love him or her. I lift up this precious person and his or her family into Your most loving, strong hands, praising and thanking You for Your Son. In the precious name above all names, Amen.

Sample Prayer for *You* to Pray

Dear Father, You alone are the One True God, the Creator of all things. You are all-knowing, and You are just, yet You continue to relentlessly pursue my child/children and me and shower us with Your love, and with Your presence. By the power and authority given to me by Your Son, My Savior, Jesus Christ, I declare that the enemy has no authority over my family. Your Word says, "No weapon formed against us shall prosper." I believe and stand on Your Word. I know, Lord, that the enemy comes to steal, kill, destroy, to plunder, and rob our hope, but My Lord Jesus came to give us life and give it to us abundantly. Lord, please bind the enemy from the destruction he has already set in motion. I know there is victory in Christ, that by His blood we are already forgiven and healed. You forgive all of our sin, You heal all of our diseases, You redeem us from the pit, and You crown us with Your love and compassion. You give us good desires and You restore us. I bring my family into Your presence to wash away every accusation the enemy has brought forth to Your throne concerning us. I bind any demonic influence that holds any of my children in bondage, blinding them or preventing them in any way from receiving their Savior Jesus. I come with confidence that You will bring forth salvation to my family for Your glory. I welcome with thanksgiving the work You will do in their lives and thank you for the answers to the many prayers that come before You for this family. In Jesus' name, Amen.

CHAPTER 9

Open *Your* Eyes and Lead Them Not Into Temptation

My children, with whom I am again in labor until Christ is formed in you (Galatians 4:19 NASB).

There's an old saying, *curiosity kills the cat*. Curiosity can ultimately endanger your child if you do not prepare her to safely process or deal with the information she gleans, if you are not around to debrief her, if she does not have a clear set of boundaries and values, if her self-esteem is low, if she is too immature to resist the temptation of experimentation, or if she has too much independence for her own good. For instance, to leave a child or youth alone with a computer is like giving a toddler a lighted match and a rag soaked in lighter fluid. Children today are logging in to find answers to some of their biggest questions. I wonder, are we simply not talking to our children about issues, are we not telling them the truth, are we minimizing the dangers, have we just resolved to give our children free reign, or are we ignorant of the facts, too tired to try, not technologically or current-event savvy? I'm not sure.

A recent study provides some scary data. If ever there was a clearer and more alarming picture of all that is going on in children's lives and hearts today, the results concerning their top Website searches, divided by age, is it. The most shocking of all of these findings are what the *youngest ones* are searching for. Brace yourself mamma and papa bear, it ain't oatmeal!

Alarming Stats

In 2009, Symantec published data from a free search monitoring service for parents (Norton Safety Minder: onlinefamily. norton) listing the top 100 Internet searches by youth 18 and under. It gives us much insight into the temptations and lures, priorities and preferences, habits and addictions of our children. "Porn" is the fourth most popular word search among children *7 and younger.* Among the findings, "sex" ranked #4 for teens and tweens while "porn" ranked overall #5 for boys, #24 for girls. The program itself, Norton Safety Minder, was the 48th most searched phrase among the children with search results providing instructions for *temporarily disabling* the monitoring program.[58] And you thought your child was an angel!

What Your Kids *May* Be Into

The top three Internet searches among all age groups were YouTube, Facebook, and Google. The first two are social networking sites where our children interact live or communicate back and forth with friends and other contacts. The sixth most popular search term for teens was "porn." Teens and tweens most often search online for music-related subjects. Kids under 7 mostly search for games. Girls are more inclined to search for social networking sites, music, or for entertainment and celebrity information. In the study, boys' top search terms were comprised of social networking sites, shopping sites (what are they buying?), inappropriate terms, and gaming.

Kids 7 and under are also into: Club Penguin, Webkinz, games, Miniclip, Nic Jr., Gmail, Cartoon Network, Poptropica, Michael Jackson, eBay, Disney Channel, Cbeebies, Hotmail, Hannah Montana, Lego, Disney, MySpace, Yahoo Mail.

Tweens are also into: Club Penguin, Miniclip, Yahoo, eBay, Michael Jackson, Fred, Webkinz, Wikipedia, Miley Cyrus, Gmail, Party in the USA, games, Taylor Swift, Addicting games, Hotmail, Poptropica, MySpace, Hannah Montana.

Teens are also into: MySpace, Yahoo, eBay, Wikipedia, Taylor Swift, Party in the USA, Michael Jackson, Lady Gaga, Miley Cyrus, Justin Bieber, Lil Wayne, Hotmail, New Moon.

What You Should Do Now: It behooves us all to figure out who Lady Gaga[59] is! You will also want to set rules about Internet use, and set appropriate parental controls, online filters, and Web search boundaries, especially to protect your child from sexual child predators and cyber bullies. There is enough information out there for you to research what works best for you, your system, and your children. Don't delay. And while you are at it, get knowledge. What lyrics are in the music your children listen to? What's the hot new video game and its rating? Who do they know online? How are Hannah Montana or Britney Spears doing these days?

The Internet

The Internet is a dangerous place for youth. Protect your children by taking these steps:[60]

1. Install an Internet filter (see Resources), blocking all chat rooms for children 16 years of age and under. Also block file-sharing programs, because they often automatically download porn or computer viruses. Some to watch for are Kazaa, BearShare, and Limewire.

2. Place the computer in the family room or kitchen, or in a place where you can see the screen as you pass by.

3. Create boundaries and rules concerning Internet use, and post them for your child to see.

4. Review Internet browsing history. For most Web browsers, hold down Ctrl and press "H" at the same time for history, or click on the History button of your browser. Most Internet filters have a feature that lets you know what sites have been visited, which cannot be erased by your tech-savvy children, as the history feature can be. Check recent documents for files transferred or received or accessed. Surf together with your child and get to know his favorite Websites and how he or she interacts online.

5. Lead by example. Trust me, your children are hawk-like! Commit to safe and healthy Web surfing yourself. Your media choices can affect your children. It is your responsibility to prevent their exposure to pornographic, sexually provocative, violent material, and online predators. It doesn't stop at the Internet. You need to be diligent in protecting them from such content on television, cell phone graphics, videos, magazines and books, and radio as well.

FREE Parental Monitoring Control Programs

The following Websites were current as of the date of this writing; however, an Internet search will show you organizations that provide this service free of charge.

Tech Mission's *Safe Families,* a nonprofit organization, offers free Internet filtering software downloadable from their Website. They also offer a free Family Pledge to print and post by your computer, which each child signs and agrees to, as well as a Media Sobriety Covenant for Adults. The site also has many tutorials as well as an online safety workshop for parents and excellent information concerning porn addiction. Visit: www.safefamilies.org.

K9 Web Protection from Blue Coat is a member of the Internet Watch Foundation, the UK Internet Hotline for the public to report their inadvertent exposure to online child sexual abuse content hosted anywhere in the world. A free Internet filtering and control solution for the home that puts the parent in control of the Internet. Visit: www.k9webprotection.com.

AOL Parental Controls claims to keep your children safer online as you set limits, choose content, and decide who can communicate with your children. It monitors their online activity when using IM's, email, and Web browsing. The software is free and downloadable from their site. Check them out at parentalcontrols. aol.com.

Increase the Likelihood of "NO"

I set about immunizing DS against drugs, alcohol, smoking, substance abuse, vagrancy, promiscuity, vandalism, unsupervised parties, and questionable Web surfing early, in age appropriate manners, of course! It is best to give children the facts before they are tempted. Those who are not properly informed are at greater risk of experimenting. It is our responsibility to research the things that daily assault our children and their temptations. Even if a child makes an effort to avoid something, even with proper guidance, he may be lured into a dangerous activity. My son had an online predator posing as a 10-year-old in an online game—that I was monitoring! We can pray, hope, and equip our children with sound knowledge, common sense, and firm resolve to make sound decisions beforehand.

What You Can Do Now: Keep tabs on your child's whereabouts. Know the parents of your child's friends. Have your child regularly check-in while out. Discuss and even act out ways to say *"no"* in response to peer pressure. Encourage your child to walk away from friends who do not respect his reasons for not engaging in dangerous, questionable, or unwise activity. Clearly state your own expectations and establish consequences for breaking the rules. Appeal to your child's self-respect, let her know she is too smart and has too much going for her to abuse a substance or engage in wrong activity. Inform your child about the dangers associated with alcohol and drugs—drinking and driving, increased vulnerability to sexual assault, greater likelihood of unprotected sex, illegal activity, harming self or others, impaired judgment, and more danger on social networking sites and while Web surfing.

Straight Up: Your values and attitudes count with your child, although you may not see it in their demeanor.

What to Do if Your Child Slips

DS played a trick on me recently. He told me he loved rum. Freaked me out! Not funny. I tried not to react, but honestly, the thought shook me up. If your older child does experiment with alcohol, a drug, cigarettes, or engages in destructive behavior, nip it, pronto, short of hauling him off to the woodshed or grounding him or her for life! What I find with DS is that it is better to ask the million dollar question, "Why did you do it?" before determining, threatening, or administering the appropriate and just consequence; otherwise, he just clams up. Be nonjudgmental, assertive but gentle, and emotionally supportive, because aggressive confrontation tends to further isolate the young person from the family bosom and the healing talk.

Then probe to discover the pattern that led your child to a "yes." What was the appeal? Was there undue pressure? Did she try to resist? Where did she get it? (prayerfully, *not* from the other parent!). Who was with her? Determine her repentance level—if low, it is serious and a much deeper problem. If high, you have something to work with right away. Resist a lecture, sermon, or preachiness, as I'm doing here! Let her know that you are trying to understand, that you want to equip her to say "no" or resist the next time.

Creating a Victory Plan

It helps me to better understand my child's triggers and willingness to work on a challenge and set up an overcoming plan if I have knowledge about the situation, because knowledge is power to overcome. Wait until you and your child are calm for best results. You may want to tailor your gathering of knowledge somewhat in a way that works best for you and your child, or use one or two approaches.

First, if I need information from DS concerning misbehavior, I probe for a source. Was the source of the temptation internal, meaning, was the flesh in operation? If so, I know it was an inside job, the flesh playing peek-a-boo with DS's mind. The flesh is so weak! This is, "I just couldn't help myself."

The problem might also be the enemy messing with DS's eyes, what we know as "the lust of the eyes." We all have this curiosity of adventure, the desire to know, the impulse to check something out, to see what something is like, to see how it tastes, to see how it makes us react, or to see if it is really not good. Oh man. I remember my first cigarette, and my thoughts about it. "I'll just take one drag to see how it tastes, what its like."

It might also be an external source—pride luring him in to do wrong, the desire for self or social acceptance or to impress someone, or to get kudos or points for something compelling him to sin. An, "I'll have a cigarette to fit in."

Second, I try to find a pattern. What did he hope to gain? What was the appeal? Motivation? What road did he travel to his "yes"? Was there an underlying problem? Loneliness? Fatigue? Insecurity? Failure? And did he try to resist? Was he pressured? Forced?

Now, armed with knowledge, I seek to see how much he understands about his actions. Unless he understands the worst that could have happened and its consequences, he cannot apply wisdom for the next time.

When I am convinced he has a sound understanding of his error, I examine his heart. Is he repentant? Sorry? Regretting his choice? Or is he apathetic, in a "puh, what-*ev*-er" mood? Is he blaming someone else? A situation? A circumstance? Me? Does he even appear upset? Is his body language saying, "I am really sorry for what I did; I won't do it again?" Or, is it telling me, "I'll just tell Mom what she wants to hear so she'll get out of my face." Unless he is repentant, he cannot possibly make a sound or believable commitment, nor can we develop an overcoming strategy.

I stop at this point for a while to pray and reassess, going over the knowledge I've gathered concerning source and pattern, and determining ways to encourage him out of the grey zone. There really is no such thing as conditional morality. The Bible is clear on what sin is and is not. Your child may struggle to determine what he has done is wrong. Until he gets into the white zone and believes that his misbehavior was not OK with no middle ground, he will not be able to resist temptation and turn from it in the future. With us, there is no grey. Something is either wrong or right. If God says DS can resist any trials and temptation,[61] I know that he can. The thing is to convince DS of it.

After he does repent, we move on to commitment. I offer my support, involvement, and reinforce my love. I assess if he needs more help than I can give, and offer it to him so that we can achieve victory. This might be the added support of a mentor, school counselor, pastor, Sunday School teacher, his father, or a peer who has been through and overcame something similar. It could be additional research or calling upon prayer warriors or intercessors to stand in the gap for him.

Finally, we cement his resolve in prayer together, and I also encourage him to take it to God himself. Then we create the plan. I review it daily for success and all of the benefits of doing right. Daily, I affirm, "With God, you can do anything!"

In forming the plan, we immediately shut the door to temptation, get rid of the access point, and seek ways to avoid the pattern and the entry points that originally lured him in. For instance, after a sleepover at a friend's house when he was much younger, he came home cussing like crazy. The sleepover was the access point for the sin. For a time, it was wiser that he did not return to this situation, at least until he had more tools to resist bending in to peer pressure. At the same time that he works on overcoming, I work on the underlying issues, because the source is the entry point for healing. Is there a place I can build him up? Is he feeling insecure? Lonely? In need of something deeper than what I see? Where is he vulnerable? Does he need outside counseling?

Many parents make the mistake of not monitoring their child's progress adequately. Don't be afraid to ask him often how he is doing in the overcoming department, especially if you share custody and he is away from you. That way, it won't have time to grow as large again. And to keep temptation at bay, I encourage DS to reaffirm his commitment and to declare that he can do all things with God's strength. I ask him to remember past victories and be grateful for them. I remind him of his successes and his future. And if he thinks he might fall into temptation again, to cry out to God and to me for help—we will both come running! If he fails, I encourage him to get right back up again, loving him through the process seventy times seven if I have to!

Help! My Children Won't Behave!

Not too long ago, a mother shared how inadequate she felt because she could not convince her children to behave. "I feel I've failed as a mother."

Who's telling her that or making her feel that way? Her child? Her ex? Unless she is truly messing up—neglecting or abusing her children, or setting them up for the pits of hell, I'd say she is doing a good job. And, if she is doing her very best parenting God's way, which is Love's way, she is doing a brilliant job. Time to get out the Mr. Clean and deal with that trashy devil and his lies!

Parenting is all about leaving a godly impression and not necessarily about our skill with a lasso. Before you brand yourself a failure, ask God, "How am I doing?" I think you will be pleased with His response. We don't see what God sees—He has a much higher vantage point. There are things happening in the supernatural of which we are unaware. God may be using the very behaviors you are trying to change in a child to turn her toward Himself His way and in His time.

I often felt like a failure when DS misbehaved or had a problem. This would place me in a funk, causing me to second-guess my best efforts and wonder if I was even fit to tie his shoes. However, we must understand that children are imperfect, and that their problems and misbehaviors are part of their life experiences. Even the only Perfect Parent, God the Father, saw His children, Adam and Eve, disobey; so for us, it is inevitable.

> **Model Moment:** Activate God's Word in your life. Memorize appropriate Bible verses—having God's Word at the ready means you have the power and wisdom of God at a moment's notice in any situation. If your child tells you, "Dad, I can't help it," you can speak to that discouragement. "Discouragement be gone in Jesus' name. Jimmy can do *all* things through Christ who gives him strength." Your child can do it because Jesus says he can. This is a great example to your child of weaving God's Word into every negative situation for positive benefit and into positive situations for positive benefit! As a result, their faith and confidence grow—yours too. As you study God's Word together as a family, ask Him to show you what He wants you to learn from each verse and how to apply it to your lives. Whatever you do, don't use the Word to berate or scare your child away from God. In all things, use the First Corinthians 13 approach—in perfect love.

Testing Limits

Occasionally DS tests my limits to see what he can get away with, and it often seems to happen when I'm on a deadline, on the telephone, or when I've just put on a wet coat of nail polish. His father and I parent two completely different ways, so perhaps his occasional misbehaviors are testing grounds to see how far he can go before *I* lose it or inflict the appropriate consequence. I can almost see his mind whirring, "Hmmm, Mom's a pushover compared to Dad!"

As tempting as it is to give in just once, stick to your house rules, behavioral guidelines, and originally set consequences. Your child will one day respect you for it. It may be worth a look at a deeper cause. What else is she going through right now? Is she having difficulty adjusting to a new school? Is she going back and forth between families? Is she resenting her dad's new girlfriend? She may be at an age where she is feeling her oats toward independence. It might be wise to encourage a new hobby, sport, or activity, or help her find a community project or volunteer work. She may be ready to take on more responsibility around the house. That's it! Get her tired enough… nah, enslaving our children is not the answer. *You* know what your child needs. God sends all babies with a recipe.

Did I mention that DS is tall for 13? He's no little green sprout, for sure. Facing misbehavior without fear can be a challenge, especially when the child in question can take me out with a flick of his Xbox controller. I trust that will not happen, but times do arise when I simply dread misbehavior, overreact, or lose it, and we get into a yelling match. Rebellion can do that. A mother can only take so many "puh, what-e-vers," you know? Usually my reaction or lack thereof is fear motivated. Not trembly fear or fear for my life, but a fear of overreacting or caving in. I have since learned that counting to a million, reading a calming Psalm, or remembering how much bigger God is than the Jolly Green Giant goes a long way toward helping me effectively guide DS.

The "No Buts" Clause

When DS was young, I taught him to be responsible and fully accountable for misbehavior to help him segue into his teen years. I prefer the "no buts" clause, which reduces the likelihood of ongoing drama, lies, excuses, bribes, or shifting blame. Mind you, there is a wee addendum attached in the event he truly was forced into a situation and had no choice, for instance, at the hands of a bully or under unbearable threat— or if the bribe is *really* good…. Other than that, there simply are no excuses.

If I'm wrong, I'll repent and make it up to the poor little fellow. He knows I give good gifts. It helps to gain knowledge that will help you both gain better understanding of the motivations and triggers and reduce the probability of error on your part and a trip to Best Buy. Remember, misbehaviors are stepping stones of growth, opportunities to learn from mistakes, so rejoice! Your child's misbehavior is also a learning opportunity for you. If God says that perseverance must finish its work so that you can be mature and complete, not lacking anything, believe it! You too are growing.[62] So resist the urge to call forth doom, as in, "You will end up in the East River like your Uncle Vinnie," and instead, call forth your child's incredible destiny.

CHAPTER 10

Big Fires From Little Sparks—
Dealing With the Tough Stuff

It's our job to build confident young people who make good choices, especially because single-parented children tend toward independence earlier than most. We want them to become good decision makers, developing the courage, resilience, and resolve to make good choices. When DS is on his own, married with children, and I'm 102 and no longer able to care for myself, I don't want him sending me to Shady Acres, if you know what I mean. Of course, the reasons why children need to prepare and develop sound decision-making muscle early are infinitely more serious.

Beware of Cookies?

Just as I was preparing this chapter, a distraught friend called to tell me that his 15-year-old granddaughter had been caught selling marijuana-laced cookies at her high school, the very same school DS will be attending next year. "Adrianna" had been "dealing" for over a month, making batches in her mom and step-dad's kitchen. She was selling each "treat" for five bucks a pop, and apparently had quite a little business going on with the students in grades 9 and 10.

The police visited her at school, charged her, and the school expelled her—forever. She hasn't yet been before a judge, but because she was caught, they enforced the zero-tolerance rule. If she wants to complete high school, her parents will have to homeschool her or provide a full-time tutor. She was charged, and here in Canada, even though she is a minor, her record may follow her into adulthood because of the seriousness of the crime of selling drugs to children.

> *I never even thought to tell DS to beware of girls selling cookies.*

She had a thriving business, which means that many children made wrong choices, possibly dozens of times. Likely this was an introduction to drugs for some, irresistibly packaged, too good to pass up. It's scary. I never even thought to tell DS to beware of girls selling cookies. Would your child buy a cookie? What if that drug dealer was in elementary school?

Perils of Negative Media Influence

The former president of a news station said that the station's job was to give people not what they want but what they (the media) decide they ought to have.[63] What if the media decides to give the impression that drugs, premarital sex, and outer perfection are the norm? Welcome to the 21st century, folks!

When our children enter middle school and high school—no, wait, *elementary* school—thinking that certain behaviors such as homosexuality and promiscuity are normal, it is in large part due to the structural sin of mass media. I remember DS at only 5 years of age asking, "Is that what teens do?" Until he was 10, he was afraid of teens. "I never want to be a teen, Mom."

Many of the things that are not good for our children are packaged to make them seem harmless. Man, do we have a fight on our hands! Too many of our children do not use their internal value systems to shape their decisions, and if they haven't any, or worse, they've adopted media's value system. Well Houston, whoa, we do have a challenge.

Media, not parents, reflect and create the culture, and if it is portraying the craziest aspects of life—what are our kids thinking? Girls as young as 7 are becoming anorexic "model" potential. Drug dealers are in elementary schools. Our children need to know that mass media has a specific agenda. They need to have reasons to stick to their values and ideals rather than allow themselves to be shaped by negative influences. How can they process what they see? Can they decipher the messages sent by media and be taught how external messages shape internal perspectives?

Power Up: A host of biblically based information is available on the Web and through churches and community resources concerning drugs, alcohol, smoking, substance abuse, sexual promiscuity, and other very real threats and concerns. I come alongside you believing that your child will not give in to the pressures or fall victim. It is our job to be informed, inform our children, equip, train, and empower them to resist temptation, to know the signs, the pitfalls, consequences, and dangers. God commands us to train them in the way they should go, but does not guarantee they will go in the right direction. Because just as you have free will, so does your young person.

What Can Your Child Grasp?

As a toddler, DS was not ready for all the facts, but I did start to develop his decision-making and problem-solving skills for the later challenges. For instance, I let him know that I trusted him to make good decisions, by letting him choose what to wear in the morning or which apple to buy at the supermarket. I had to set an example, as well, so from time to time I would let him see me make decisions that were good for me, such as not eating a fifth piece of apple pie. This showed him that although something looks appealing, it isn't necessarily good for you!

At age 6 and 7, DS lived in the present. "Later," held no meaning to him. He had little grasp of space and time. At this stage, he relied on present experience (touch the stove, it burns you), so I took advantage of teachable moments. For instance, walking by a group of teens smoking, I would talk about nicotine addiction and what it does to a person's body and health, or why teens smoke to look cool. Sometimes this led to additional questions and discussions. Specifics did not seem to bother him. For instance, I told him what could happen in the event of a drug overdose, and shared with him about a friend's daughter who was a heroin addict and in the hospital, and the sadness it brought her parents. I recall we were listening to a news report about a family's home being vandalized, and this prompted a discussion about feelings, and hurting people. Right then, he vowed never to vandalize property, and to this day, he has never intentionally done so, except for my diamond watch down the toilet, but he really thought it would float!

When DS was between ages 8 and 12, he loved weird facts, world record books, and "how did they do that" stuff. He wanted to know how things worked and why, and why people behave the way they do, which seems indicative of this age group. This was a good time to ask him how he felt about things like drugs, alcohol, and sex because he did not suspect this as interrogation, as he would at age 13! It is surprising what he already knew—stuff that I did not tell him. Shocker! However, at these ages, he was still open to talking about it. Thus, I established dialogue as often as I could. "What do you think about drinking?" "Has anyone ever offered you a sip of beer?" Now that he is a teen, he clams up more often.

Don't be afraid to ask sensitive questions. Your question concerning harmful substances, behaviors, or unhealthy curiosity may not immediately result in a discussion, but it gets your child thinking about things and at least shows him that you are open to the topic and willing to hear what he has to say about it. Springboard into discussion using current events, news headlines, and things you both hear about, like the teen down the street's joy-ride arrest. At this age, DS's friends had more influence on him, thus his interests sometimes were determined by what his peers were into. Like Xbox. This is the time to teach your child to say "no" to negative pressures and to discuss how vital it is to stick to values and ideals and who they are as individuals. Oh, and while you're at it, do a little digging into their friends' pastimes.

When DS turned 13, things really changed, and I found myself wishing I had taken more discussion time with him than I did. Here is where all of those things we discussed became reality in his surroundings: drugs, alcohol, and his increased sexual awareness. Thankfully, he is still willing to tell me about it, or alert me to it. This is where I find it vital to understand his thoughts, concerns, and feelings about deep issues, resisting the urge to say, "If I ever catch you…." Also, this is the age where he knows both his limits and boundaries, and my feelings, beliefs, and expectations about abstinence and responsible behavior.

Daily, I reinforce what I have been teaching him all along in a way that keeps the doors of communication open, without threats, without preaching, (most of the time!) and for sure from a foundation of love rather than a dictatorship. I am fully aware that this increasingly independent stage is ripe for defiance of my rules and wishes, particularly as he uses leverage to get back at his dad or me. However, I continuously try to help him feel accepted, respected, and never fearful of coming to me about anything. This has increased the likelihood that he will continue to be open with me. Just the other day, DS asked me about marijuana for medical use…ouch, and I was as calm (not!) as a cucumber about to be pickled.

Conclusion

Miraculously, flying solo has been my greatest opportunity to deepen my own spirituality through the tears, the very real fears, and the inevitable mistakes I make and will make in the struggle to be a good parent. Consequently, that makes me a better parent. I *am* moving forward, making progress and improvements along the way, although I may not be where I want to go now. Some days seem slower going, but overall I am making headway. And you will too!

"The beauty of parenthood…," a friend counseled during one of my first meltdowns and right after I'd spent the better part of the evening scrubbing poop off the walls of DS's room, "…is that it is as much for you as it is for your son." I thought my pal daft and did not appreciate him upsetting my pity party like that. But I understand it now because, my oh my, how the Master Potter has shaped, chiseled, and molded me. I have seriously grown in my spiritual walk, learning to lean on Jesus and trust in Him. During the process, my son and I have grown more than when we depended on another person for our needs.

When you see yourself from God's perspective, from heavenly places, you see the big picture, which makes it that much easier to move forward. Learn to view your life from that eternal perspective, because the current moment is so small, finite, and absolute in comparison!

Parenting is about eternity, about God causing all things to work together for your good. It is an ongoing process, line upon line, until one day you will see the fullness. Trust that your efforts, even your mistakes, are all used in the grand masterpiece!

You may not have received all that you ordered for your life plan, but cherish what you do have. Awaken to the excitement of being a parent, the reality of God's exciting presence in your home, and His extravagant miracle-working power in your life. Keep in touch with your heavenly Parent—if you lose sight of Him, you will come undone!

His presence in your home will not only influence your children when they walk through the door after school, but also enables them to live for God when independent of your direct influence.

As I've said, parenting is not about perfection, it's about embracing and treasuring the perfect love of God, and parenting from that most valuable reality, mirroring the profound relationship you have with the Lord. As your children find their way toward their own faith, you will all grow in perfect fearless love to conquer every enemy potshot! May I remind you one last time? God simply asks, of all of us, "Did you parent today in love?"

Endnotes

1. Dorothy Leigh Sayers, writer, poet, Christian humanist, 1893-1957.

2. See Jeremiah 29:11.

3. Proverbs 22:6.

4. See Luke 12:34.

5. See Genesis 2:22-24; 4:1-2.

6. Please read Nehemiah chapters 1-2, where the prophet Nehemiah gives an account of his grief when he discovered the great affliction that had fallen upon the Jews and of the broken city of Jerusalem. You will relate!

7. See Jeremiah 18:1-6.

8. See Matthew 6:8b,31-34.

9. For Scriptures on God's desire to make us whole, please read *The Message* translation of the Bible: First Thessalonians 5:23; John 3:16; 10:10.

10. See First Peter 2:20-25.

11. See Luke 23:34.

12. See Mark 7:20-23.

13. Larry Walker, "Discover the Power of Forgiveness," *Virtual Christian Magazine* (United Church of God, 2003), http://www.vcmagazine.org/article.aspx?volume=05&issue=01&article=forgiveness (accessed April 23, 2010).

14. Rick Warren, *The Purpose-Driven Life: What on Earth am I Here For?* (Grand Rapids, MI: Zondervan, 2002), 90.

15. Don Nori Sr., Publisher, Destiny Image Publishers, quoted from a ministry post. Used by permission.

16. Matthew 6:33, emphasis mine.

17. Barbara Yoder, author of *Taking on Goliath,* Website: www.shekinahchurch.org. Used by permission.

18. See Titus 3:4-5.

19. Read John 11, particularly verses 17-27 and 38-44.

20. "Chillax," a blend of "chill out" and "relax." *The Urban Dictionary,* www.urbandictionary.com (accessed December 18, 2009).

21. See First Corinthians 15:14.

22. Adapted from *The Message Bible,* Romans 12:2.

23. See John 15:5-8.

24. See Colossians 3:1-4.

25. *"Let your life shine before men…"* (see Matt. 5:16).

26. See Philippians 4:6.

27. John 16:20.

28. See Philippians 4:13.

29. See Isaiah 40:8.

30. See John 11:11-45.

31. See Zechariah 4:6.

32. See Ezekiel 36:25-27.

33. See Philippines 3:9-11.

34. The findings were presented at the British Psychological Society annual conference in Brighton and reported by Telegraph.co.uk: "Having tattoos like David Beckham 'is a sign of low self-esteem'" by Kate Devlin, published 12:01AM BST 03 Apr 2009 (accessed November 1, 2009) http://www.telegraph.co.uk/science/5095591/Having-tattoos-like-David-Beckham-is-a-sign-of-low-self-esteem.html.

35. Lorrie Blair, "Tattoos & Teenagers: An Art Educator's Response," Art Education, v60, n5, p39-44 Sept. 2007; Education Resources Information Center; accessed Nov. 20, 2009; http://www.eric.ed.gov:80/ERICWebPortal/custom/portlets/recordDetails/detailmini.jsp?_nfpb=true&_&ERICExtSearch_SearchValue_0=EJ774986&ERICExtSearch_SearchType_0=no&accno=EJ774986.

36. See First Corinthians 15:32. All of First Corinthians 15 is devoted to the hope of the bodily resurrection of believers in Jesus and His atoning sacrifice on the Cross. Paul, in his letter to the Corinthians, was trying to emphasize the idea through analogy that contending for the faith would be in vain

without the hope of bodily resurrection, for without that hope there is no faith to contend for. If there was no resurrection, people might as well live like the Ephesians, giving in to human passions.

37. See Second Corinthians 1:8-9.

38. See Second Corinthians 5:14-15; Hebrews 2:9; First John 2:2.

39. An unknown author quoting Angus H. Strong in *Systematic Theology*.

40. See Psalm 22:10.

41. See Psalm 71:6.

42. See Isaiah 46:3.

43. See Genesis 17:10-14; Leviticus 12:3.

44. See Luke 1:41,44.

45. See Luke 1:5.

46. See First John 4:4.

47. "It Has to Happen Faith" is the power of Christ inside you and your children. Meditate on the following verses (yes, you have to open the Manual for Life yourself), and ask God to transform this knowledge of His power into "It Has to Happen Faith." See Psalm 66:3; 68:35; Micah 3:8; Matthew 8:16-17; 9:6-8; Luke 9:1-6; 10:19-20; Acts 1:7; Romans 8:37; 8:9-11; First Corinthians 4:20; Ephesians 1:19-23; 6:10-12; Philippians 3:10-11.

48. Audrey Meisner, *It's a New Day*, May 2009 Newsletter, www.newday.org.

49. Don Nori Sr., Publisher, Destiny Image Publishers, quoted from a ministry post on Facebook. Used by permission.

50. Mother Teresa, *Church News,* October 24, 1992, p. 2.

51. Read Psalm 4:3.

52. Adapted from an article by Robert Brooks, Ph.D., "How Can Parents Spot Low Self-Esteem in Their Children?" posted on www.greatschools.net (accessed January 9, 2010).

53. From a variety of personal interviews, experiences, and sources, including: Healthy Place, America's Health Channel at http://www.healthyplace.com/depression/children/risk-factors-for-child-and-teen-suicide/menu-id-68/.

54. See Psalm 127:3.

55. Sarah Palin in a video interview with the Billy Graham Evangelistic Association. (BGEA); http://www.billygrahm.org/News_Article.asp?ArticleID=730 (accessed January 8, 2010).

56. For further study about praying over your home, read Deuteronomy 6:6-9; 20:5; Joshua 24:16; Second Samuel 6; Proverbs 24:3-4; Psalm 127:1.

57. Quote by Cornelius Plantinga Jr.

58. "Top 100 Kids' Online Search Words for 2009" (Churchrelevance.com, 2010); http://churchrelevance.com/top-100-kids-online-search-words-for-2009/ (accessed January 1, 2010). Also found at OnlineFamily.Norton, http://onlinefamilyinfo.norton.com/articles/kidsearches_2009.php (accessed May 9, 2010).

59. Research Lady Gaga yourself—I simply have no words to describe her. When you see her photo, you will know why the kids are into her.

60. Adapted from article, "Safety Steps and Rules for On-line Safety for Parents to Protect their Children" at www.safe-families.org/safetysteps.php (accessed January 9, 2010).

61. See First Corinthians 10:13.

62. Perseverance; see James 1:2-4.

63.

Suggested Resources

The following resources—books and Websites—are provided to help you research and gain knowledge about subjects that arise and that are important when raising children in our modern age. Just remember, line everything up with God's Word, trust the leading of the Holy Spirit and His discernment, and pray for wisdom as you seek additional counseling or helps.

Your number one single parenting resource is the Bible. You will be surprised to discover how practical and encouraging it is for parents. If you could have only one parenting book, the Bible is it! For starters, Genesis tells the story of Adam and Eve and their perfect Father and encourages you that even if you were the perfect parent, your children could still make wrong choices.

It is also a great bedtime story book filled with true tales of adventure, romance, supernatural feats, heroism, and the impossible made possible, and, it is compelling, inspiring, awesome and terrifying at the same time! The stories are vivid of real people facing real problems and overcoming! It is a treasure of morals, virtue, and resolve to do what is right at all cost. It teaches the Golden Rule, and shows our children how consequences good or bad help to shape and grow us into God's good and perfect plans and purposes. It teaches our children about destiny, and the very real one God has for His children. Most of all, it teaches that failure does not have to be permanent, and this is encouraging especially to the single parent and single parented child. The most worn book in my house is the Bible and my favorite parenting helps are found in the Books of Proverbs, Psalms, First and Second Corinthians, and Ephesians. Ground yourself in His Word, and you will have firm footing in all of your research!

Website Disclaimer:

Websites and content can change quickly. Some may be hacked or hijacked and the site owner may not be aware of it. Parents, always first visit a site before recommending it to your child. If it is interactive, be certain to monitor your child's activity.

Chapter 1

Revolutionary Parenting: What the Research Shows Really Works by George Barna

Chapter 2

Make Room for Your Miracle: Releasing Resurrection Power in Your Life by Mahesh and Bonnie Chavda

The Mom I Want to Be: Rising Above Your Past to Give Your Kids a Great Future by T. Suzanne Eller

Healing Rooms Ministries: A free resource, sometimes by love gift. Ministry teams gather in Healing Rooms across North America and in many countries of the world to pray with you personally for your specific needs and healing in emotional, spiritual, and physical areas of challenge. This free resource has been of great encouragement to my family. Call ahead and book a time, or just drop in when they are open. Call, visit their Website, or email for a list of locations and hours of operation in your community. Telephone: 1-509-456-0517; Website: www.healingrooms.com; email: healing@healingrooms.com.

Chapter 3

The Dangerous Book for Boys by Conn Iggulden and Hal Iggulden

Strong Fathers, Strong Daughters: 10 Secrets Every Father Should Know by Margaret J. Meeker

Better Dads, Stronger Sons: How Fathers Can Guide Boys to Become Men of Character by Rick Johnson

Boys Should Be Boys: 7 Secrets to Raising Healthy Sons by Margaret J. Meeker

What a Daughter Needs From Her Dad: How a Man Prepares His Daughter for Life by Michael P. Farris

Loving Our Kids on Purpose: Making a Heart-To-Heart Connection by Danny Silk

The Five Love Languages of Teenagers by Gary Chapman, Ph.D. and Ross Campbell, M.D.

Five Signs of a Loving Family by Gary Chapman

Heartfelt Discipline: The Gentle Art of Training and Guiding Your Child by Clay Clarkson

The Ultimate Win/Win: Communicating Love to Your Family by Rabbi Moshe Goldberger

The Christian Mom's Idea Book: Hundreds of Ideas, Tips, and Activities to Help You Be a Great Mom by Ellen Banks Elwell

Chapter 4

Suite101.com articles posted under "Christian Parenting" offer many interesting free ideas regarding helping children deal with grief and loss, including age-appropriate conversations with children about death, helping children readjust, heal, and manage their grief and worries while at school.

Chapter 5

Family Devotional Builder: Devotional Resources for Elementary-Age Children and Their Parents by Karen H. Whiting

The Heart of Anger: Practical Help for the Prevention and Cure of Anger in Children by Lou Peril

Learn the *slanguage*. Get savvy; communication goes both ways! If you don't understand your youth's gobbledegook, it is possible he is using slanguage, youth speak. You can find a rather extensive slang dictionary at www.thesource4ym.com/; (the source for youth ministry). Some words are clever and amusing, but the Website warns that some meanings and definitions can be shocking or crass regarding drug, sex, violent, or criminal behavior. However, they did their best to edit while preserving the true meaning of the words. They recommend that you use discretion.

Chapter 6

Kingdom Parenting by Dr. Myles Munroe and David Burrows

What Manner of Child Shall This Be: How to Influence Your Child's Destiny by Dr. Rex Obeng

The 7 Habits of Highly Effective Families by Stephen R. Covey

A Life of Miracles: A 365-Day Guide to Prayer and Miracles by Bill Johnson

Chapter 7

The Power of a Praying Parent by Stormie Omartian shares how you can pray through every age and stage of your son or daughter's life, and includes sample prayers.

The Gift of Being Grand by Marianne Richmond

Shepherding a Child's Heart by Tedd Tripp

Raising Kids to Love Jesus by H. Norman Wright and Gary J. Oliver

Why Christian Kids Leave the Faith by Tom Bisset

The Power of a Positive Mom by Karol Ladd

Raising Respectful Children in a Disrespectful World by Jill M. Rigby

www.christianteens.net —A source of fun and information for Christian teens and adults.

superbook.cbn.com —Superbook Kids Website is a safe place for your children to play free online games, learn more about the Bible, and grow in their faith.

www.streetbrand.com—A Christian teen magazine and Christian youth Website with a Christian teen social network.

www.christianitytoday.com—An online Christian magazine with tons of self-help articles and forums.

www.christianyouthweb.com —For youth, strong on music and missions, has a video room.

www.christiankidstop100.com —Christian Kids lists the top 100 fun Websites, researched and rated by kids for kids. Sites that are Mom-approved. Lists the best places on the Web for Christian children to visit for fun, games, learning, and devotions. Not all sites are solely Christian but they indicate all are safe and fun.

Chapter 8

Frank Hammond Books:

Manual for Children's Deliverance
Demons and Deliverance
Overcoming Rejection
The Breaking of Curses
Pigs in the Parlor

Derek Prince Books:

They Shall Expel Demons: What You Need to Know about Demons: Your Invisible Enemies
Blessing or Curse: You Can Choose
Entering the Presence of God
Secrets of a Prayer Warrior
Does Your Tongue Need Healing?
Rules of Engagement: Preparing for Your Role in the Spiritual Battle
Bought with Blood: The Divine Exchange at the Cross

Chapter 9

An excellent parenting resource is Linda Massey Weddle's *How to Raise a Modern-Day Joseph: A Practical Guide for Growing Great Kids*. She describes how parents can intentionally plan the best itinerary for their children's spiritual journey from birth through high school. She gives specific steps in raising children to have an enduring faith in Christ, with family spiritual goals and a super Bible reading plan for family devotions.

The Blessings of a Skinned Knee: Using Jewish Teachings to Raise Self-Reliant Kids by Wendy Mogel, Ph.D.

Awana: Each week more than a million children and youth ages 2 to 18 participate in Awana, a program of ministries offered in over 1,800 churches in the U.S. and internationally. These programs change young lives through biblical truth. Awana Clubs are weekly programs. 24 Ministries are for middle and high school. Awana Lifeline is a ministry for children of inmates. Awana International is a global ministry for children and youth. Visit www.awana.org to locate a ministry near you.

*Don't Make Me Count to Three! A Mom's Look at Heart-Oriented Disciplin*e by Ginger Plowman

Good and Angry: Exchanging Frustration for Character in You and Your Kids by Scott Turansky and Joanne Miller

Gospel-Powered Parenting: How the Gospel Shapes and Transforms Parenting by William P. Farley

Boundaries with Teens: When to Say Yes, How to Say No by John Sims Townsend

Note From the Author

And one more thing...

You have just finished reading the first in the Single Parent series of books. *The Single Parent's Guide to Raising Godly Children* is a God-incident, so don't relegate it to serendipity or chance. This is a divine connection of single parents purposing in our hearts to settle ourselves so that we can settle our families God's way. As such, this book, as you have discovered, is as much about you as it is about your children.

This first volume is the longest one in the series, because knowing God and learning how to overcome in His power is key to everything we attempt. Thus, laying a godly foundation eases us into other core issues. In future books, Lord willing and with your support and feedback, we will deepen and sharpen our focus on practical key daily concerns, the current and greatest challenges. I welcome your response and opinions, and invite you to write or email:

singleparentguide@gmail.com

or write to:

Shae Cooke
ᶜ/₀ PO Box 78006
Port Coquitlam, B.C.
Canada, V3B 7H5

Also visit my Website, **www.shaecooke.com**
It links you to my single parenting blog and other resources!